CHECKMATE!

The Wonderful World of Chess

FSC
www.fsc.org
MIX
Paper | Supporting
responsible forestry
FSC® C020056

This book is mainly dedicated to all those children I've taught and from whom I have learned so much.—JF

Published in 2023 by Mortimer Children's
An Imprint of Welbeck Children's Limited,
part of the Welbeck Publishing Group
Offices in: London - 20 Mortimer Street, London W1T 3JW
& Sydney - Level 17, 207 Kent St, Sydney NSW 2000 Australia
www.welbeckpublishing.com

Author: John Foley
Design: Darren Jordan and RockJaw Creative
Design Manager: Matt Drew
Editorial Manager: Joff Brown
Production: Melanie Robertson

ISBN: 978 1 83935 248 5

Printed in Heshan, China

10 9 8 7 6 5 4 3 2 1

CHECKMATE!

The Wonderful World of Chess

JOHN FOLEY

MORTIMER

CONTENTS

FOREWORD 6

LET'S PLAY 8

THE HISTORY OF CHESS 10

SETTING UP THE CHESSBOARD 12

HOW TO READ A CHESS GAME 14

MINIGAMES 16

THE CHESS PIECES

    The Pawn 18

    The Bishop 20

    The Rook 22

    The King 26

    The Queen 28

    The Knight 30

SPECIAL MOVES 34

TRICKY TACTICS 38

ATTACK & DEFENSE 46

CHECK & CHECKMATE 56

OPENINGS 64

STRATEGY 72

ENDGAMES 80

THE TOUCH MOVE RULE 88

USING A CHESS CLOCK 89

CHESS TOURNAMENTS 90

CHESS & TECHNOLOGY 96

SHIROV v POLGÁR 102

GLOSSARY 106

ACKNOWLEDGMENTS 112

FOREWORD

The first time that I introduce chess to a group of children, I explain to them that they can regard the chess set as a board with 32 inert pieces, or it can be a magic world to enter.

My purpose is to give them a glimpse of how the pieces can come to life, how the game is rich and subtle. Not least, I want them to know how fun and exciting it is to join the chess world. I am keen to be their guide.

The book *Checkmate! The Wonderful World of Chess* by John Foley makes me feel superfluous because here all my goals are fulfilled in written form. With a pedagogic approach based on years of experience, mixed with entertaining facts in an attractive layout, this book will not only make the beginner take the first steps towards mastery, but also give him or her a real chance to fall in love with the game.

You have just opened the door by starting to read this book. Please enter. Welcome to the wonderful world of chess!

Jesper Bergmark Hall

FIDE Senior Trainer
Chairman, Education Commission, European Chess Union

LET'S PLAY

Welcome to the world of chess! Chess is a great game which millions of people around the world enjoy. It is an ancient game, but it never feels old. The basic rules are easy to learn, and you can start playing right away.

Age doesn't matter—a 6-year-old can play a 60-year-old! You can play with friends and family. You can play with a board, or online. You can play at home, at school, at a club, or in the park. You can play when you travel, and in any countries you visit. All you need is a board and a set of pieces.

Chess is exciting to play. You must try to outwit your opponent. You strive to find moves to set them problems. How can I improve my position? Where are my weaknesses? What is my opponent trying to do? These are the thoughts that run through your head when you play chess. People who play chess like to solve problems. They enjoy the satisfaction of finding the only move which wins, or saves, the game. This requires concentration, logical analysis, finding patterns, and the ability to control emotions.

When you win a game of chess, you'll feel good. You have achieved something. A game has two people struggling to win with an uncertain result until the very end. It's fun to overcome a tough opponent, rather than have an easy victory. It's natural to get a bit nervous when playing, but with practice and preparation you become more confident and can start to be successful.

Remember—even the best chess players make mistakes and lose from time to time. Nobody likes losing, but it's part of life. Chess teaches you to accept defeat graciously. You know what it feels like to lose, so when you win, please show respect to your opponent. For example, mention how close the game was and how it could have turned out differently if they had played another move.

Wherever you go in the world, you can meet other people with a shared interest in chess. You have a common language. There is no other game so widely played. Let's start your chess journey—turn the page to find out how to begin!

Advanced Tip

The best advice to improve your chess is to play, play, play. Play as much as you can. The more you play, the better you'll get!

THE HISTORY OF CHESS

Chess is an ancient game invented in India. It was taken up by the Persians around 1,500 years ago. In fact, the word "Checkmate" comes from the Persian language and means "The king is helpless"!

Chess reached Spain around a thousand years ago, then spread throughout Europe, where the rules were modernized into those we play today. In England, the chess pieces were named according to roles in medieval society. The king and queen were supported by the church (the bishops) and the cavalry (knights) with the castles (rooks) in the corners. The farmers (pawns), who were the soldiers in those days, marched into battle.

In the 1800s, chess was played in cafés where the chess masters would earn money by beating challengers. By the 1920s, chess was popular all around the world, inspired by the World Champions José Capablanca and Alexander Alekhine. The International Chess Federation (FIDE) was established in 1924, which runs the Chess Olympiad every two years. The USA won in 1931, 1933, 1935, 1937, 1976, and 2016—a level of success second only to Russia. When Bobby Fischer won the World Championship in 1972, it was a way to show that Americans could beat the Russians at their own game.

Today, computers can calculate moves better than humans, helping us get better at chess. We can play anytime with other people from around the world. Just think—thousands of games are being played online right now.

This means that the new generation of young chess players is the strongest in history. Books on chess are better, training is better, chess software is better, and more games are being played than ever. Children are playing better than ever before. Some children even become a grandmaster at the age of 14. Maybe you'll be next!

The word "checkered" comes from chess!

Champions of Chess

The current world chess champion is Magnus Carlsen from Norway **(right)**, who gained the title when he was age 22. Other young winners include Garry Kasparov at 22 and Mikhail Tal at 23. Russian players used to dominate world chess, until Bobby Fischer became the only American to be world chess champion in 1972.

The first women's World Chess Championship was won by Moscow-born Vera Menchik in 1927. Russia and Georgia were once the dominant countries in women's chess, but Ukraine and China have caught up. Some of the top women players, like Judit Polgár from Hungary, did not compete in women's events because they felt that men and women are equal in chess.

There are also world chess championships in other categories such as by age (under 8, 10, 12, 14, 16, 18) or by playing speed.

WORLD CHESS CHAMPIONS

2013	–	now	Magnus Carlsen	Norway	
2007	–	2013	Viswanathan Anand	India	
2000	–	2007	Vladimir Kramnik	Russia	
1985	–	2000	Garry Kasparov	USSR/Russia	
1975	–	1985	Anatoly Karpov	USSR	
1972	–	1975	Bobby Fischer	USA	
1969	–	1972	Boris Spassky	USSR	
1963	–	1969	Tigran Petrosian	USSR	
1961	–	1963	Mikhail Botvinnik	USSR	
1960	–	1961	Mikhail Tal	USSR	
1958	–	1960	Mikhail Botvinnik	USSR	
1957	–	1958	Vasily Smyslov	USSR	
1948	–	1957	Mikhail Botvinnik	USSR	
1937	–	1946	Alexander Alekhine	France	
1935	–	1937	Max Euwe	Netherlands	
1927	–	1935	Alexander Alekhine	USSR	
1921	–	1927	José Capablanca	Cuba	
1894	–	1921	Emanuel Lasker	Germany	
1886	–	1894	Wilhelm Steinitz	Austria	

SETTING UP THE CHESSBOARD

Before you start, it's important to know how to set up your pieces.

Getting started

Always position your board so that the bottom right-hand side of the board is white. The same pieces start opposite each other. For white, the king is on your right hand side; for black, the king is on your left hand side. The queens are on the d-file; the white queen is on a white square and the black queen is on a black square.

Naming the squares

Each square has its own letter and a number. The letter is along the bottom and the number is along the side. The vertical lines are called **files**, and the horizontal ones are called **rows** or **ranks**.

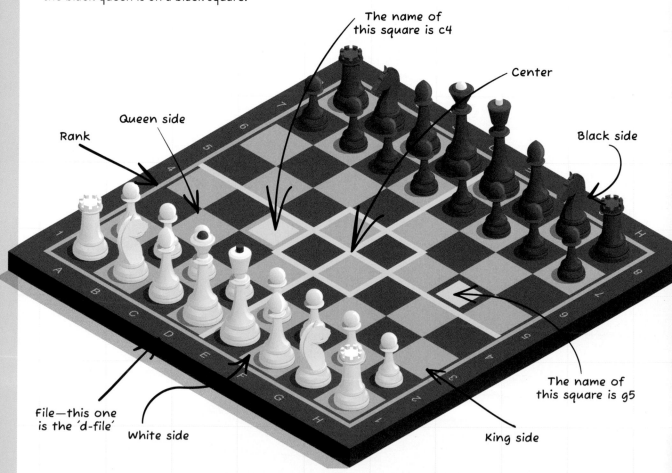

The name of this square is c4

Center

Black side

Rank

Queen side

File—this one is the 'd-file'

White side

King side

The name of this square is g5

How the diagrams work

Here's how to understand all the chess diagrams in this book.

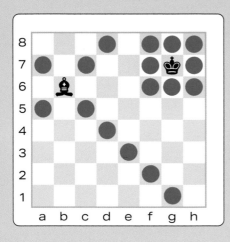

◄ The green circles show all the squares a piece could move to—its **move pattern**.

➡ The blue arrows show a piece **move**.

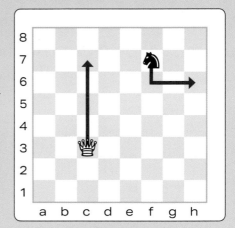

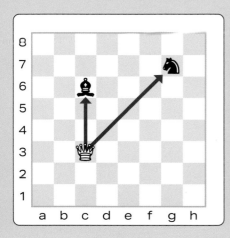

◄ The red arrows show a **threat**. The attacking piece can capture the threatened piece!

➡ The green squares are **safe,** and the red squares are **unsafe**. Here, the king can't move to the red squares because they are **under attack**.

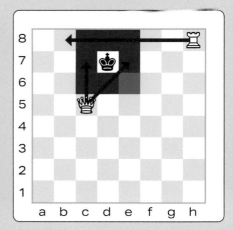

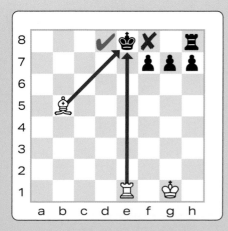

◄ The square marked with a red cross is a **bad move**. The square marked with a green tick is a **good move**!

➡ The green arrows show where a piece **protects** another. The red arrows show where a piece **attacks** another.

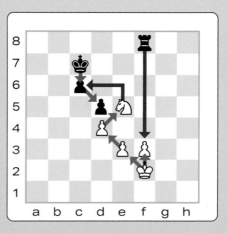

H::W T:: :E::: A CHESS GAME

We know the moves of chess games played hundreds of years ago, because the moves were written down. This way, great games can be studied and talked about forever.

As you read through this book, you'll find some games described by a series of letters and numbers. Here's how to read them...

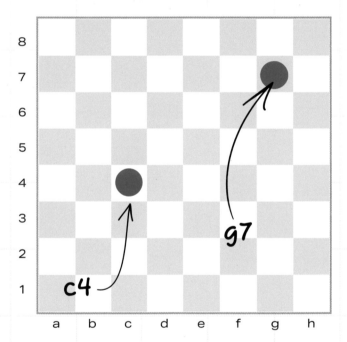

Coordinates

Every square on a chessboard has a name given by its coordinates as seen from White's point of view.

The **c4** square is on the c-file and the 4th row.

The **g7** square is on the g-file and the 7th row.

Remember **"along the corridor and up the stairs."** Start with moving along the bottom to the right until you find the letter corresponding to the file you want. Then move up until you find the row you want.

Pieces

Each piece is assigned a single letter.

 King = **K**   Bishop = **B**

 Queen = **Q**   Knight = **N** (the K is already used for the king, so the knight uses the second letter!)

 Rook = **R**   Pawn = **the file (column) it's on**

Moves

Each move is numbered, so the notation **1.d4 c5** means that on the first move, White played a pawn to **d4** (it moved the d-pawn two squares forward), and Black responded by playing a pawn to **c5** (it also moved the c-pawn two squares forward). Captures are signified by an "x", so **2.dxc5** means that the white pawn on **d4** has captured the black pawn on **c5**.

A move is signified according to where the piece moves to, so **2...Qa5+** means that on its second move, Black played the queen to **a5**. We do not need to write down where it came from, because there is only one possibility. A "+" symbol means that the move gives check. The symbol for checkmate is "#".

Special moves

Castle kingside (short castling)	**0-0**
Castle queenside (long castling)	**0-0-0**
Promotion	**h8(Q)**
En passant	**axb3 e.p.**

The position after **1.d4 c5 2.dxc5 Qa5+ 3.Nc3 Qxc5**

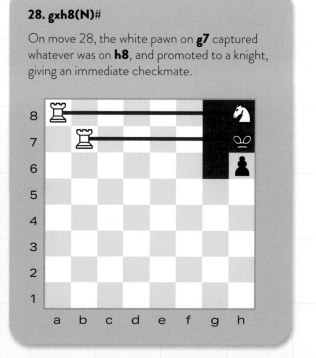

3.Nc3 Qxc5 means that White moved its knight to **c3** to block the check and then Black captured the pawn on **c5**.

promote to a queen on the **h8** square

the pawn advancing from **b2** to **b4** was captured on **b4** by the black pawn on **a4**

The notation can combine these elements together:

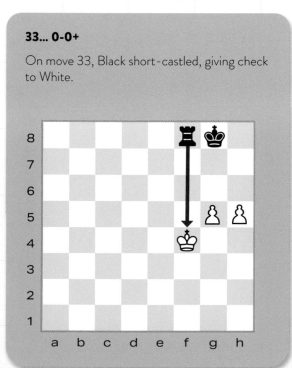

33... 0-0+

On move 33, Black short-castled, giving check to White.

28. gxh8(N)#

On move 28, the white pawn on **g7** captured whatever was on **h8**, and promoted to a knight, giving an immediate checkmate.

MINIGAMES

The best way to learn chess is to start simple!
These fun minigames will help teach you some basics.

Fox & Hounds

RULES: In this simple minigame, all pieces can move one square diagonally on the dark squares. The lone fox (white) goes first. He can move forward or backward, but the hounds (black) can only move forward. The fox wins by reaching the opposite side. The hounds win by blocking the fox so it cannot move. You can't capture any pieces, or jump over them.

Players take turns to move one piece at a time. Let 's look at a game...

Fox and Hounds game starting position

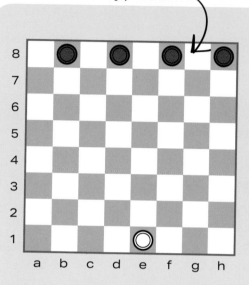

1 The fox has moved from **e1** to **d2**. It now has a choice of four moves marked by blue arrows. One hound at **h8** has moved to **g7**. The hounds can only move forward to the squares marked with green arrows.

The game continues with each player taking a turn to move.

Position after one move

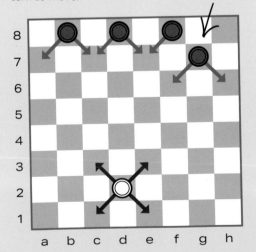

2 Let's skip ahead a bit. The fox has gone as far forward as it can, and is blocked by the hounds. The player with the hounds has to decide which move to play...

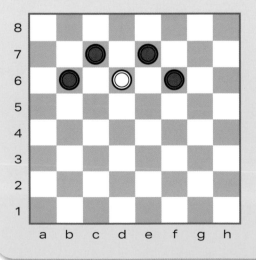

3 If a hound moves outward to **a5** or **g5** (marked by green arrows) then the fox will be able to break through.

Suppose the hound moves **f6-g5**, this leaves a gap at **f6**. The fox will move **d6-e5,** aiming for the gap.

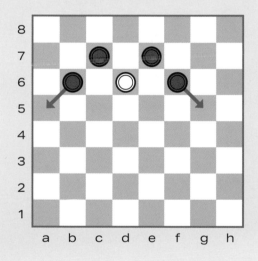

4 Even if the hound on **e7** tries to cover the gap, the fox will double back and get through to the opposite side via **e7**.

Hounds can't move backward, so the hound on **f6** cannot move back. The fox wins this game!

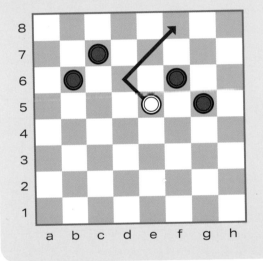

5 If you play perfectly, the hounds should always win. The secret to winning is to keep the hounds in formation as they zigzag down the board. The best chance for the fox is to disrupt this formation, and force the opponent to think. The fox can only win if the hounds make a mistake—and it's easy to make a mistake in this game!

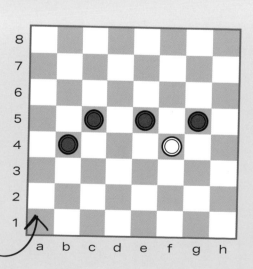

The hounds have a winning formation

THE CHESS PIECES

Get to know the moves, rules, and quirks of all the pieces on the board.

The Pawn ♟

The pawns are like the soldiers in chess. They may seem weak, but they're crucial to victory!

1 Each player has **eight pawns**. Pawns **can't move backward**.

On its **first move**, a pawn can move **one or two squares forward**. On all other moves, it can only move **one square forward**.

Here, you can see that White moved their pawn two squares to **c4**. Black moved one square to **e6**.

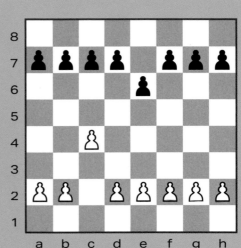

2 A pawn can only capture **one square diagonally forward**. (Pawns are the only pieces to capture differently to how they move.) A captured piece is removed from the board.

The pawn at **c4** can capture the one on **d5**. The pawn at **d5** can capture the one on **c4**.

Remember, a pieces doesn't have to capture another piece if you don't want it to.

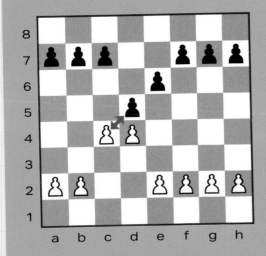

3 If a pawn reaches the other end of the board, it is **promoted to (changed into) another piece**. To promote, replace the pawn on the final rank with a new piece. Usually, you should promote to a queen because this is the most powerful piece!

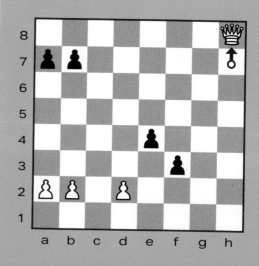

The Pawns Game

Here's a minigame which just uses the pawns. The winner is the person whose pawn reaches the opposite end first. White goes first. Playing this game will help you learn about how pawns move, capture, and defend themselves. Here is an extract from a game...

The Pawns Game starting position

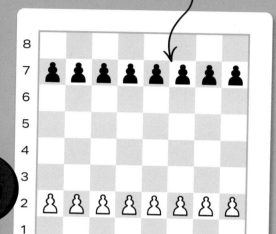

Learning chess with minigames is easier, and you learn something new each time you play. Practice these games until you are confident to play them.

1   Black has just played **d7**-**d5**, threatening White's pawn on **d4**. If white captures by **d4xe5** then Black will have two connected pawns in the center. These are dangerous, because Black can advance the **e5** pawn and if it is captured by the pawn on **f3**, then Black can recapture with the pawn on **d5**. Then the d-pawn cannot be stopped from promoting.

2   There is no way to stop the pawn on **d4** from reaching the end of the board—Black wins!

To avoid this situation, white should have played a different move earlier in the game, even before the previous diagram.

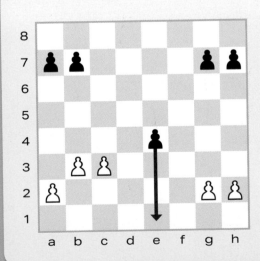

The Bishop

The bishops are the fast runners in chess! They move quickly along the diagonals and can cover both sides of the board. Each bishop can only move on squares of the same color. You start with two bishops, one of each color.

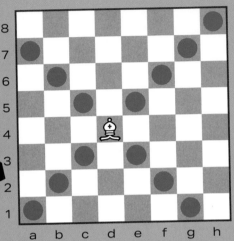

1 The bishop can **only move diagonally**. It moves **as many squares as you want.** A bishop always runs on the **same color squares.**

2 A bishop can **capture an enemy piece which is in the way.** It can be **blocked by a piece from its own army.**

Here, we see that the bishop can't attack **a1** or **g1**—there are white pieces in its way. The bishop can capture either the pawn at **a7** or the pawn at **f6**.

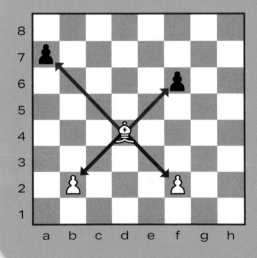

3 The bishop is a long distance piece and can be used to stop pawns from reaching the end of the board and promoting to queen.

Here the black pawn on **e2** is about to promote on **e1**. **Bh4** stops the e-pawn from promoting... but then Black will play **d3-d2** and the d-pawn will promote on d1. The only move to stop both black pawns from promoting is **Bc3** which controls the **a5-e1** diagonal.

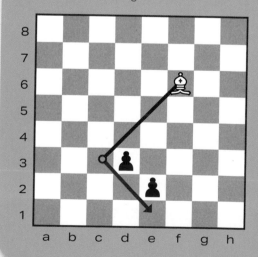

20

The Bishop vs. Pawns Game

This game shows you how to advance pawns so that they protect each other. The bishop tries to control the diagonal in front of the pawns, which must proceed quickly but cautiously.

RULES:

Players move alternately. Pawns go first. The pawns win one reaches the other end safely. The bishop wins by capturing all the pawns.

Let's look at a couple of game positions...

The Bishop vs. Pawns Game starting position

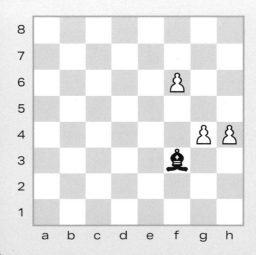

1   In this game, Black has just played the bishop to **g6**. This sets a trap for the pawns. Whether the **a-pawn** or the **c-pawn** moves, it will be captured. It is unavoidable that at least one pawn will be lost. After that, the next two pawns will not survive long enough to reach the end.

2   In this game, the black bishop is attacking the pawn on **g4**. However, the bishop does not have time to capture the pawn because the pawn on **f6** will advance to **f7** and cannot be prevented from reaching the end. The bishop can only attack pawns on white squares. Hence a pawn that reaches a black square will be safe.

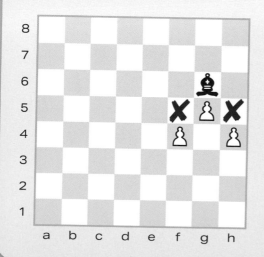

The Rook ♜

The rook is a powerful piece, especially when two rooks are linked together. Rooks can control and invade a file (vertical line of squares), and start attacking from behind enemy lines.

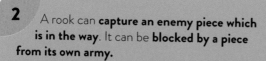

Rooks often give checkmate! The most basic checkmate pattern to learn is with king and rook against a king.

1 Each player starts with two rooks. The rook moves **up, down, right, or left** as many squares as you want.

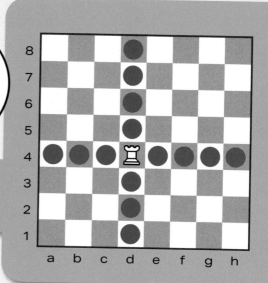

2 A rook can **capture an enemy piece which is in the way**. It can be **blocked by a piece from its own army.**

This rook can't reach **a4** or **b4** because it is blocked by its own bishop. The rook can't reach **d1** or **h4** either, because it is blocked by its own pawns. The rook can capture the black pawn on **d7**.

3 If the rook moves forward to **d7**, it is happy because it can capture one of the pawns — either on **e7** or on **f7**.

However, the rook should not move to **d6**, because it can be captured by the pawn on **e7**.

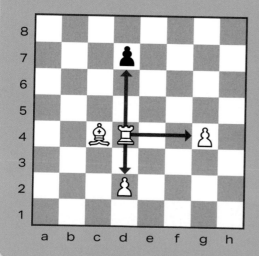

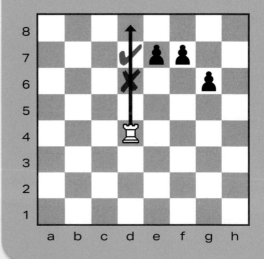

The Rook vs. Pawns game

The Rook vs. Pawns Game shows you that an effective way to capture pawns is from the side, and that the best way to catch passed pawns is from behind.

RULES

The player with the pawns goes first. The pawns are coming down the board. The rook wins by capturing or blocking the pawns so none can move.

The player with the pawns wins if one reaches the other end safely.

Let's look at some game positions...

The Rook vs. Pawns Game starting position

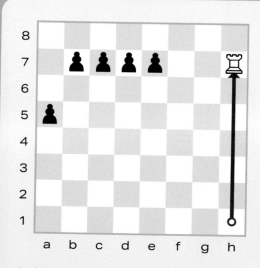

In this game, Black's first move was **a7-a5**. White moved the rook to **h7**.

Black is racing to the first rank. White is trying to capture as many pawns as possible from the side.

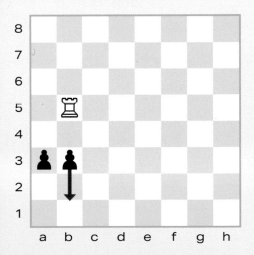

Black has managed to advance the a and b pawns to the third rank. The rook is behind them.

The winning move for Black is **b3-b2**. Whatever White then plays, Black will get a pawn through to the end!

23

The Rook vs. Bishops Game

This minigame introduces the important chess tactics of **forks** and **skewers**. Playing perfectly, you'll reach a draw, but it's easy to make mistakes if you're playing quickly.

RULES:

The bishops have the first move. You win by capturing one of your opponent's pieces.

The Rook vs. Bishops game starting position

Game on!

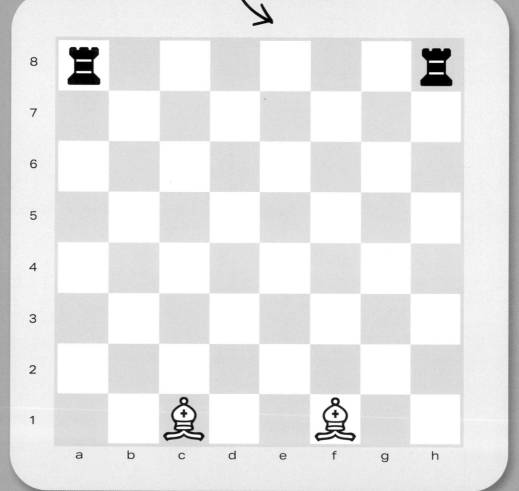

FORK

A **fork** is when you attack a piece on the same line as another piece. So if the first piece moves out of the way, you can still capture the second piece. Here, the bishop on **b2** attacks both rooks at the same time.

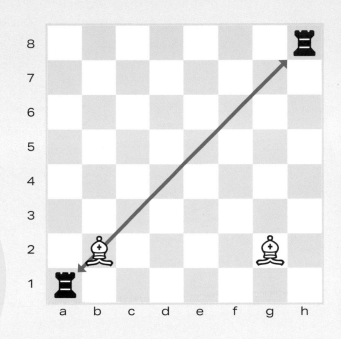

Did you know?

Rooks used to be called castles in English. The name of the piece was changed to rook because historians discovered the original name of the piece was "rukh"—a tortited chariot used in battle. The rukh piece ran up and down the board like a chariot!

SKEWER

Skewering is when you force a piece to move out of the way, letting you take another piece. If the rook on **c4** moves out of the way, the bishop on **e6** can still attack the other rook. See pages 40 and 41 for more about forks and skewers!

25

The King

The king is the most important piece. It needs to be protected because if you lose your king, you lose the game!

The king is strongest in the endgame, because it is in less danger of being checkmated.

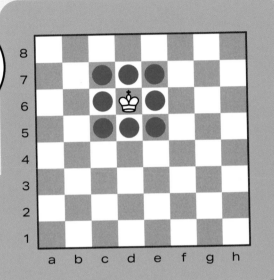

1 The king can only move **one square in any direction**.

It is the most important piece because **if your king is captured, you lose the game.**

2 Here, the king can only move to the squares marked in green, because the other squares are attacked by the rook or the bishop.

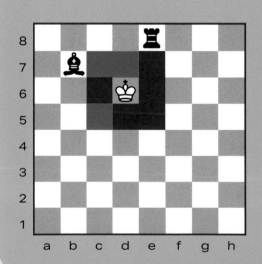

3 A king **cannot be next to the other king.**

This is the nearest that kings can get to each other!

The King and Pawns Game

This is like the Pawns Game on page 19—but with the addition of kings. The arrival of the king adds a lot more possibilities!

RULES

A king is added to its starting square behind the line of pawns. The winner is the first person to reach the other side with a pawn safely, i.e. the pawn is not immediately captured by the king. You can also win if you capture your opponent's king.

The King and Pawns Game starting position

1 Games with a symmetrical pawn formation usually end in a draw. If **1.h4xg5 h6xg5** there is deadlock with neither side able to break through.

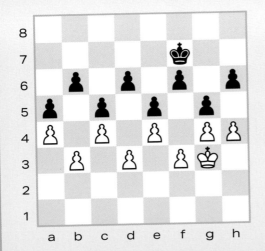

2 White should not move a pawn to any of the squares marked with a cross because it would be taken. And the king can't move to any of the marked squares because it would be in check.

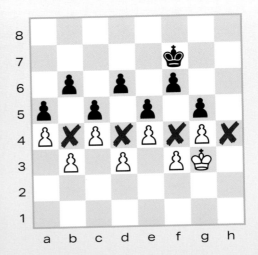

The Queen

The queen is the strongest piece and is the favorite for beginners. It can capture lots of the opponent's pieces. When pawns promote, they usually become a queen! This is why chess sets often come with two queens of each color.

> The queen is good at "forking" (attacking two pieces at once), especially pieces which are distant from each other. The queen is the easiest piece to give checkmate with.

1 The queen moves **diagonally and orthogonally (up, down, left, and right)** as many sqaures as you want. It combines the power of the rook and the bishop. It is the most powerful piece on the board.

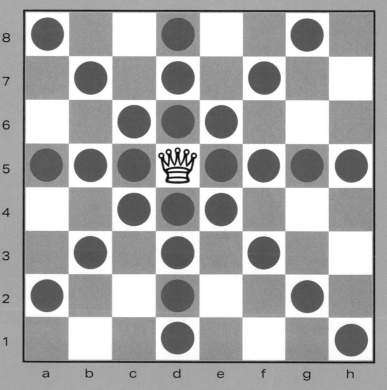

2 Here, we see that the queen cannot reach **a2** because it is blocked by its own pieces. The queen can capture one of the pawns on **a4** or **b7**, or the bishop on **g5** or the rook on **g2**.

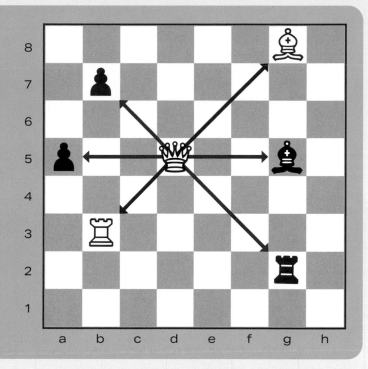

3

The queen can often attack two pieces at once. Here we see that if the queen moves to **d7** then it is attacking the rook on **c8** and the bishop on **g7**. Attacking two pieces at once is known as a fork. Forks are dangerous because the defender may not be able to defend against both threats.

The Knight ♞

The knight is the only piece that can jump over other pieces.
It moves in an "L" shape, so it can be the trickiest piece to learn.

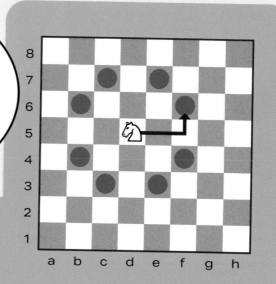

The knight is best in the center of the board, sitting on an outpost protected by a pawn. It's famous for being able to attack two or more pieces at once!

1 The knight has an **L-shaped move**: **two squares up, down, right, or left** followed by **one square to the side**.

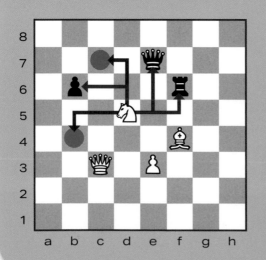

2 The knight can move to the squares marked in green. It can capture any of the black pieces on **b6**, **e7**, or **f6**. It cannot move to a square occupied by a white piece.

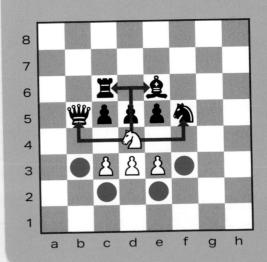

3 Here we see the knight can jump over the pawns to capture a black piece, or jump back to the squares marked in green.

The Queen vs. Knight Game

In this minigame, the knight moves first. Whoever captures the opposing piece is the winner.

The queen is powerful, but the knight dances around her like a jester in the royal court! It's all about figuring out a systematic way for the queen to win.

The Queen vs. Knight Game starting position

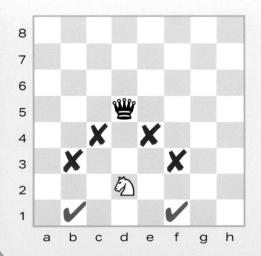

1 When the queen is next to the knight, it controls six of the eight available squares. The knight must retreat.

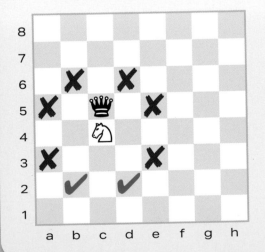

2 Let's say the knight retreats to **d2**, then the queen will continue to dominate the knight by moving to **d5**, restricting the squares available to the knight and forcing it to the edge. The closer to the edge the knight gets, the more chance the queen has to win!

Losing Chess

In this fun variant of chess, you have to lose all your pieces to win! It's a great way to become familiar with how the pieces move and interact, and it's quick to play too.

RULES

Starting with the normal board setup, the objective of the game is the reverse of chess: the first player to lose all their pieces wins the game. The rules are the same as in regular chess, but with the following changes:

- ♔ If you can make a capture, you must do it. Kings can be captured without ending the game.

- ♔ If there is more than one capture, it is your choice.

- ♔ If no moves are possible, the player with the fewer pieces is the winner.

Being forced to take pieces really makes you think ahead, which is one of the key skills in chess. A typical game takes around ten minutes. Someone who is good at chess would be good at Losing Chess; someone who loses at chess would also lose at Losing Chess!

Losing Chess Opening Moves

1.e3 b5 2.Bxb5 (forced)
Bb7 3.Bxd7 (forced)—
see the diagram. Black now has a choice of four moves. If **3...Bxg2**, White has to capture the king on **e8**.

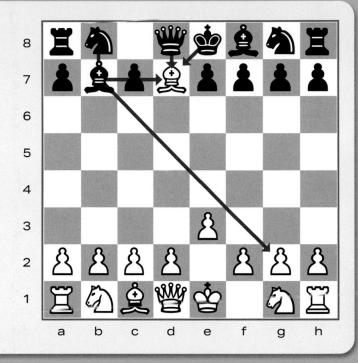

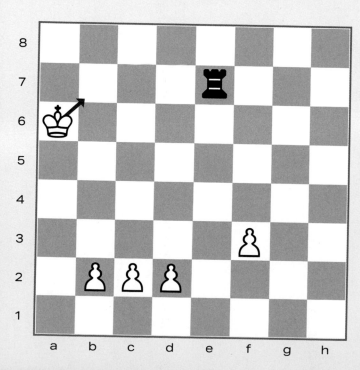

Losing Chess Endgame

In this game, although Black is down to one piece, White can still win this game with
1.Kb7 Kxb7 (forced)
2.b4 Rxb4 (forced)
3.c4 Rxc4 (forced)
4.d4 Rxd4 (forced)
5.f4 Rxf4 (forced).

33

SPE-IAL M--VE

There are three special moves in chess: castling, pawn promotion, and capturing a pawn *en passant*.

Advanced Tip

It's best to castle as early as possible so you do not fall for any tricks against your king!

Castling

Castling was invented to allow players to place their king in safety. It involves moving both a "castle" (rook) and the king in the same move. It's the only time that more than one piece can be moved.

1 The special king move called castling allows the king to move **two squares toward the rook** and then the rook **moves the other side of the king.** It is the only double move allowed in chess.

In this game, White wants its king to move from the center toward the corner of the board where it will be safer. Time for some castling...

2 ...Now the white king is safely in the corner.

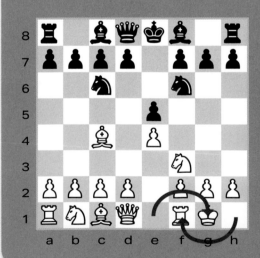

3 You can also castle on the queenside. In this game, White can castle by moving the king **two squares toward the rook** and then placing the rook on the square the king has just crossed.

4 Once White has castled on the queenside, the result looks like this.

Castling rules

Castling can only take place under certain conditions. **You cannot castle if:**

♖ There are any pieces in the way

♖ The king is in check or would be in check on the landing square (it does not matter if the rook is under attack)

♖ The king or the rook has already moved

♖ The king would have to move across a square which was under attack

The king must move before the rook, so complete the king's move before the rook's move. Be careful not to touch the rook before the king or else you will have to move the rook and cannot castle on that side. Some tournaments do not penalize you for touching the rook before the king but this needs to be announced in advance.

1 In this game, White cannot castle kingside for three reasons: the king is in check, the king would have to cross a square under attack (**f1**), and the king would land on a square under attack (**g1**).

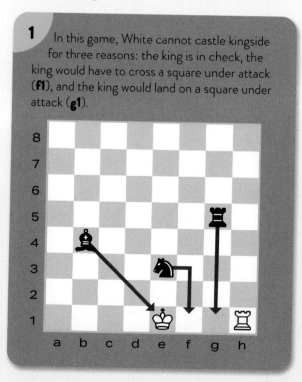

2 Here, White can castle queenside, because it does not matter if the rook or the **b1** square are under attack. The king can happily go to **c1** and the rook comes to **d1**.

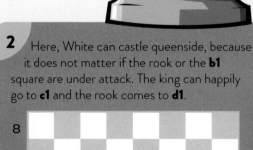

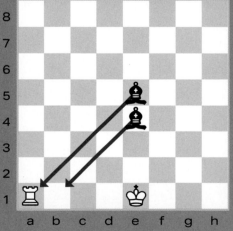

Pawn Promotion

When a pawn reaches the other side of the board, you can promote it to a queen, or any other other piece you choose. The weakest piece becomes the strongest!

Advanced Tip

Promotion can play an important part in the endgame of chess—so try to promote your pawns, or stop pawns from being promoted.

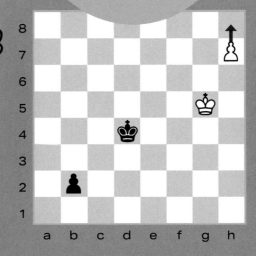

1 In this example, there has been a pawn race, with both sides wanting to promote. White reaches **h8** before Black reaches **b1**. Once the white pawn reaches **h8**, you can replace the pawn with a queen. Suddenly, the queen is giving check to the black king which must move. Then the pawn at **b2** can be captured.

2 This game looks grim for White, who is a rook behind and the white queen is under attack. However, White can set a trap. White can capture the rook and if the queen recaptures, the pawn promotes to a knight, forking the king and queen. The trap can be avoided with **Qxc4+** and seeking perpetual check.

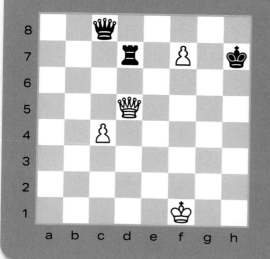

3 Here, the king must move and the knight captures the queen. After that, it is not difficult for the white king and knight to escort the c-pawn to the end to promote to a queen. The king and a knight cannot get checkmate on their own, so they need to create a queen.

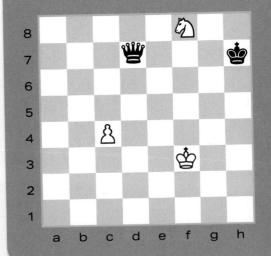

Capturing *En Passant*

We know that pawns capture diagonally one square in front of them. What happens when the opponent's pawn on its starting square advances two squares instead of one? The *en passant* rule says that you can capture this pawn "in passing" as if it had moved only one square.

The white pawns are on the fifth rank guarding the black pawns from advancing. The b-pawn has not moved. The e-pawn moves one square and can be captured by the d-pawn in the usual way. The h-pawn moves forward two squares to **h5** and gets captured *en passant* on **h6**. So you can see that it makes no difference whether the h-pawn started by moving one or two squares.

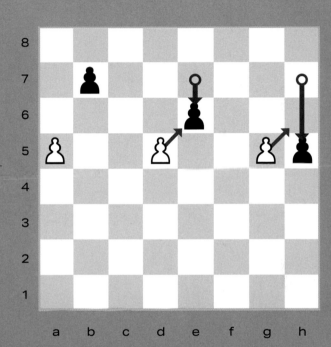

EN PASSANT RULES

♟ The *en passant* rule only applies to pawns, not to the other pieces.

♟ The white pawn must have advanced to the fifth rank and be waiting for the black pawn (or vice versa playing from the other side).

♟ *En passant* must be done immediately on that move or the opportunity passes.

♟ Capturing *en passant* is not mandatory – it is your choice whether to capture.

Did you know?

En passant was invented 500 years ago when players started moving pawns two places on their first move to speed up the game. The people still using the older rules complained that this upset all their chess plans. So it was agreed that the pawns can move forward two squares on their opening move, but they can still be captured as if they had only moved one square according to the old rules. Everybody has been happy with the rule since then... even if people have forgotten why they had it!

TRICKY TACTICS

These tactics are essential for winning pieces by exploiting a weakness in your opponent's position. The most important tactics are the "cutlery" of chess—pins, forks, and skewers!

Pins

A pin is when a piece is attacked along the same line as a piece behind it.
A pinned piece is in danger of being lost.

1 The rook moves from **f1** to **c1**, pinning the knight against the king. The knight cannot move because the king would be under attack. There is no way to protect the knight, which will be captured on the next move.

Here, the bishop moves from **e2** to **c4**, pinning the queen against the king. The bishop is protected by the rook on **c1**. Black's queen can now only move along the **c4-f7** diagonal and will be lost in exchange for a bishop.

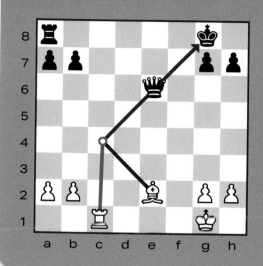

The knight is pinned against the king and so it cannot move. Therefore, the white queen can immediately capture the rook. A piece pinned against the king guards nothing.

Alternatively, here White could have captured the knight with the bishop and, after the pawn recapture, taken the rook with the queen.

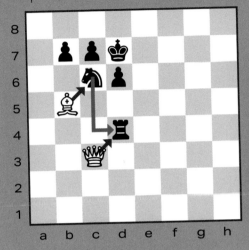

Pins against anything other than a king are not so secure, because the pinned piece can still move to deliver check or threaten mate.

The bishop is pinning the knight against the queen so normally the knight would not move. White sees a chance to get a checkmate in the corner and so moves the knight to **d6** threatening to deliver checkmate on **f7**. Black does not have time to capture the queen.

Winning a queen is not as important as winning the game.

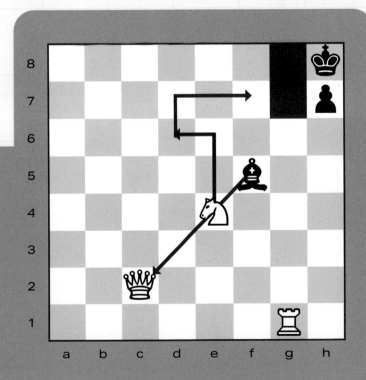

Forks

A fork is when one piece attacks two pieces at the same time. It is a common way to win a piece because usually only one piece can be saved. Forks against the king force a move, because they cannot be ignored.

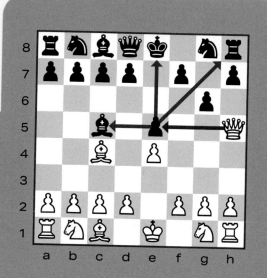

1 White was threatening checkmate on **f7** so Black pushed forward the g-pawn to **g6** to attack the queen and to block its attack on **f7**. Unfortunately, this allowed the queen to capture the pawn on **e5** with spectacular consequences.

The queen has checked the king as well as forked the rook on **h8** and the bishop on **c5**. Black cannot defend against all these attacks and will lose the rook.

2 White to move. The material is equal but White has a well-placed knight on an outpost where it cannot be attacked by a pawn or the bishop. Taking the bishop with the knight leads to an equal position. A clue in the position is that the bishop is a knight's distance away from its queen. So if White's knight could capture the bishop and give check at the same time, then it would be able to capture the queen.

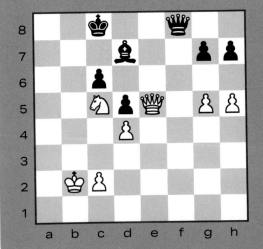

3 Amazingly, the white queen can move to **b8**, giving check to the king. The king has to take the queen. The queen has sacrificed itself to deflect the king from protecting its bishop. With the black king on **b8**, White takes the bishop with check, forking the king and the queen. At the end of this combination, Black will be a knight ahead. Forking the king and queen together is known as a royal fork.

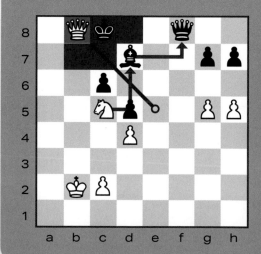

Skewers

A skewer is when one piece is under attack and has to move out of the way—revealing an attack on the piece behind it.

1 White is down on material here but has a good move to save the situation. Moving the rook to **c8** gives check and performs two skewers. Black must move his king off the back rank leaving its rook at **h8** vulnerable to capture. Even better, when the rook moves, it unblocks the bishop attack on the queen.

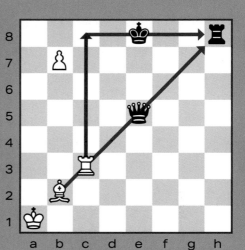

2 The black king and queen are on the same diagonal and White spots an opportunity. The white bishop moves to **e5** skewering the king and queen. If the king captures the bishop, then White's queen drops back to **c3** where it skewers the king against the queen, winning the queen.

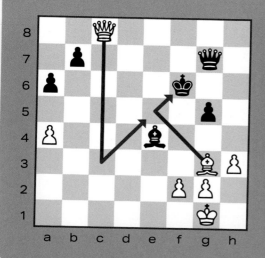

3 The sides are level in material and the pawns are symmetrical so one might expect a draw. Black's weakness is that the white queen can get around the back by playing to **f8**. This forces the king to step in front of its pawns at **f6** which is fatal because White can then check the king from behind on **h8**. The black king must move off the diagonal and the black queen has been skewered.

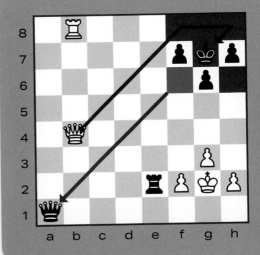

Discovered attack

A discovered attack is when a piece moves out of the way to reveal an attack from another piece. This often results in the attacker winning material.

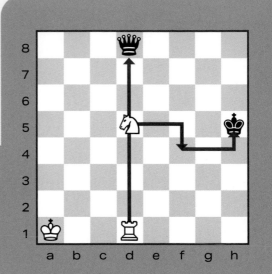

The rook can see the queen on the other side of the knight. So if the knight moves out of the way and gives check, then Black is obliged to move its king whereupon the rook can capture the queen. The discovered attack is on the queen.

Black has just captured the **d4** pawn with its queen. This is a well-known trap in the opening. The white bishop moves to **b5** giving check. Black must deal with the check and meanwhile its queen will be captured by White's queen. The discovered attack is on the queen.

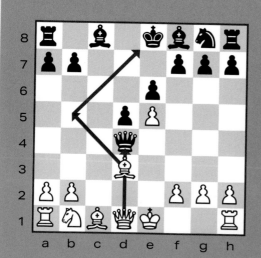

The knight jumps to **b6** giving check to the king. The escape square on **b8** is unavailable because of the bishop. So Black is forced to capture the knight with the pawn. White recaptures with the pawn, revealing a check from the rook which is in fact checkmate.

When a discovered attack is on the king, it is called a "discovered check." This is a rare example of a discovered checkmate.

Try to put your rook on the same line as your opponent's king or queen, because once the in-between pieces have cleared, you have a chance to get a discovered attack.

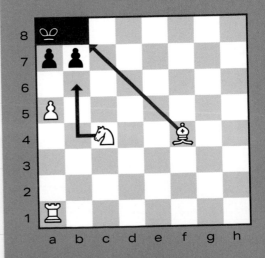

Removing the guard

If a piece is protecting a vital square, see if you can capture it, threaten it, block it, or lure it away.

1 In this example, the knight is protecting the rook from the attack by the queen. Note that the knight is under attack from the bishop and Black, to move, would capture the knight. The normal recapture of the bishop by the pawn restores the material balance. However, the queen can now capture the rook which has lost its guard.

2 The **h7** square is the target of White's bishop-queen battery. If White could capture **h7**, it would be checkmate. Presently, the knight is guarding **h7** so the correct move is to capture the knight with the rook. If Black recaptures the rook, then you get checkmate. If Black plays a defensive move such as **g6**, then you can retreat the rook having won a piece.

You have removed the knight guarding against checkmate.

3 Here the knight is defending both the rook on **e8** and the pawn on **h5**. White can win by capturing the rook and when the knight recaptures, the white queen can deliver checkmate at **f8**.

White could also win by capturing the pawn at **h5** with the queen giving check. If the knight captures the queen, then rook takes rook is checkmate.

Double attack

A double attack is a single move which makes two threats at the same time.

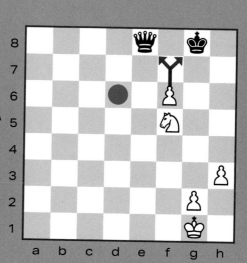

The f-pawn advances, threatening the queen and checking the king. Black is obliged to capture the pawn. If the king captures, then the knight will jump to **d6** (marked); if the queen captures, then the knight will jump to the corresponding square on **h6**, delivering a royal fork in either case.

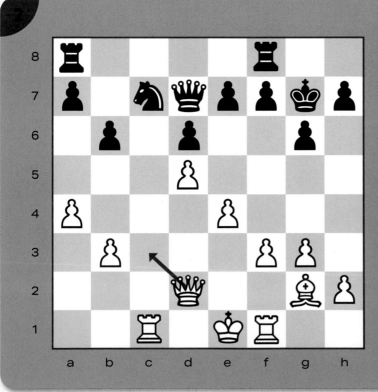

White plays the queen to **c3** which checks the king and adds a second attacker along the c-file. Black must deal with the check after which White will capture the knight at **c7** and be a piece ahead.

44

Unprotected pieces

Double attacks are particularly effective when one of the targets is an unprotected piece.

1 In this game between two former world chess champions, White finds a move which attacks two unprotected pieces. Black must lose the knight or the bishop.

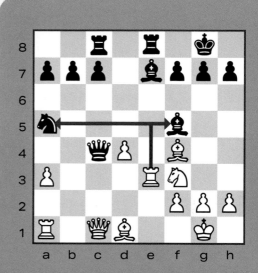

2 Here is an example from a league game. White has some weaknesses: the rook at **a1** and the pawn at **d4** are unprotected. If the bishop were not at **d6** then Black could grab the **d4** pawn. Another weakness is the pawn at **h2** which is only protected by the king. If this pawn is captured then the white king is drawn into the open. Given these clues, Black embarks on a tactical combination to win a pawn.

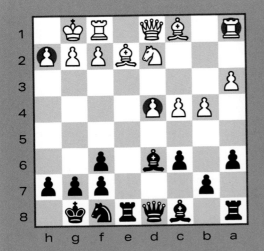

This is the position one move later when the bishop has been sacrificed on **h2**. The black queen takes the pawn at **d4**, attacking the rook in the corner. White replies by moving the knight to **b3**, defending the rook and attacking the white queen.

Now comes a double attack. The black queen moves to **e5** where it checks the king and joins with the rook to attack the bishop on **e2**. So Black gains the bishop at **e2** and ends up with an extra pawn.

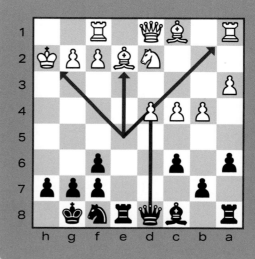

ATTA-K & DEFENSE

Chess is a bit like managing a sports team. To win consistently, you need to understand how to both attack and defend.

Piece Protection

Make sure your pieces are protected if they are under attack.

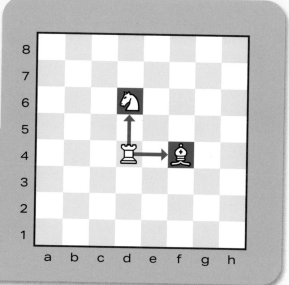

1 The rook is protecting the knight and the bishop whose squares are marked in green. If one of these pieces were captured, then the rook would recapture.

The rook is not protected. Unprotected pieces can often be attacked and lost.

2 The queen attacks the rook and knight. The knight is not worried because it is protected by the rook.

However, the rook is without protection. It is on an unprotected square marked in red. Some action must be taken or the rook will be lost.

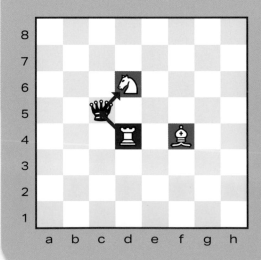

3 The rook on **b8** is attacking the white bishop on **b2**. To avoid being captured, it must move. However, nearly all the squares it can move to are unsafe, marked in red, being under attack from various black pieces. Hence, the only safe square the white bishop can move to is **a1**.

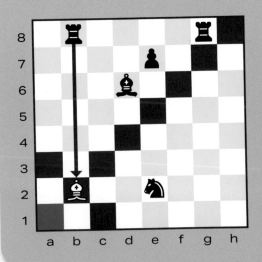

Piece Attack

The most effective attackers are pieces. They move faster than pawns, and can attack in different directions.

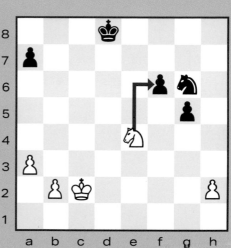

1 The white knight attacks the pawn at **f6**. Black would like to advance the pawn **f6-f5** but this would mean that the pawn at **g5** would be unprotected and would be captured.

The only way to protect the **f6** pawn is by moving the king to **e7**.

2 Attacks are more effective if you attack more than one piece at the same time—a double attack. The defender may not be able to deal with both.

Here the queen is attacking the pawns at **a7** and **g7**. Even if one of the pawns were to move out of trouble, the other one would be captured. This is a queen fork.

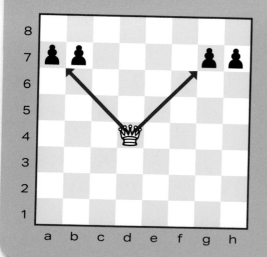

3 In this position, the knight has just moved from **c3** to **d5**. This has opened the long diagonal so that the bishop on **b2** is attacking the rook on **h8**. This is known as a discovered attack. The knight is attacking the bishop on **e7**. So two pieces are attacking two other pieces at the same time.

There is a way to defend. Black can move the rook to **e8** which gets off the diagonal and protects the bishop.

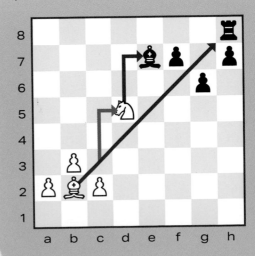

Defending against a double attack

When two of your pieces are under attack, try to find a way to move one out of trouble so it protects the other piece. Move and protect at the same time!

1 Here the knight is attacking the pawn at **c4** as well as the bishop on **g4**.

However, in this case, there is a way to defend. The bishop can retreat to **e6** protecting the pawn at **c4**.

2 Here the bishop is attacking the white rook and, if the rook gets out of the way, the knight on **f3** is under attack. It looks like White might lose a piece. Fortunately, there is a move which saves the situation. If the white rook moves to **d3**, it protects the knight.

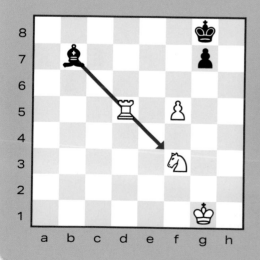

3 Here is a similar situation. The bishop is attacking the unprotected knight. If it moves, then it appears that the pawn on **g2** can be captured. There is a way to defend. If the knight moves to **f4** then it protects **g2**. This is the idea of move and protect.

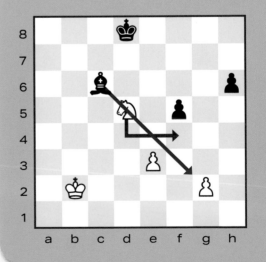

Counterattack

You can respond to a threat by making one of your own. Counterattack is often the best form of defense. In these positions, it is White to move.

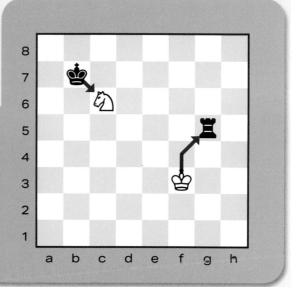

1 The white knight on **c6** is under attack from the king. White could move the knight away. Alternatively, White could advance the king to **f4** to threaten the rook. Black cannot win without this rook and so will move the rook rather than capture the knight.

2 The white bishop on **b5** is under attack from the knight. White could move the bishop from harm's way. Alternatively White could advance the g-pawn threatening the rook. The rook is worth more than the knight so Black should consider moving the rook.

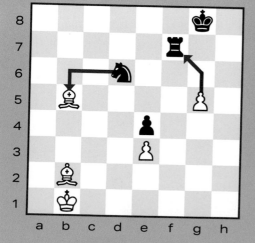

3 The white rook is under attack from the pawn at **e3**. White could move the rook to avoid being captured. Alternatively, White could advance its pawn to **g7** to counterattack the black rook. If Black then captures the white rook on **f2**, White will capture the black rook giving check. The black king must move, which gives the white queen time to stop the black pawn from reaching **f1**.

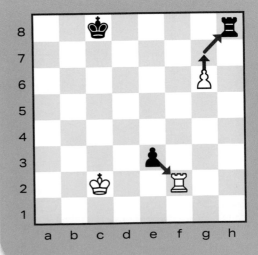

Defending your army

Keep an eye on each of the pieces, yours and your opponent's, to identify which are unprotected.

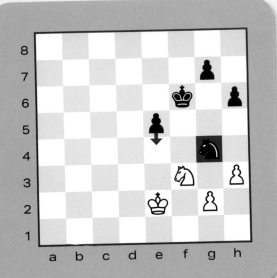

1 In this example, the black knight is attacked by the pawn and it has nowhere to escape.

There is a way out of this problem. Black can counterattack the white knight on **f3** by advancing the e-pawn. If the white knight moves, then the black knight can retreat to **e5**. If White captures the black knight, then Black will capture the white knight.

2

Whenever you look at a position, note which pieces are protected and which are unprotected. An unprotected piece can be usually captured without harm.

Here, the white pawn on **b2** can be captured by the black queen on **b6**. The queen would then also be attacking the unprotected rook on **a1**.

The value of the pieces

Each piece has a guideline exchange value measured in the equivalent number of pawns. Always aim to keep more valuable pieces in play than your opponent.

Queen  = 9 ♟♟♟♟♟♟♟♟♟

Rook = 5 ♟♟♟♟♟

Bishop = 3 ♟♟♟

Knight = 3 ♟♟♟

The queen is the strongest piece, and you should avoid exchanging it except with the other queen. The bishop and the knight, known as the minor pieces, are worth about the same. If the position is blocked with pawns, then the knight is usually stronger. In the endgame, if there are pawns on both wings, then the bishop is preferred. The rook is stronger than the minor pieces, especially in the endgame.

1   In the middlegame, a knight in the center can be stronger than the rook if it can make threats or control vital squares. The rook is often exchanged for such a knight.

Here we see an "exchange sacrifice" by a rook for a knight to disrupt the opponent's position by doubling the c-pawns. Then Black captures the **e4** pawn after which Black will play **d5** with a formidable pawn center.

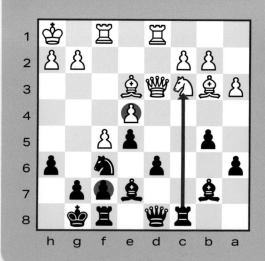

2   A rook is worth around five pawns in theory but two connected passed pawns on the 6th rank cannot be stopped—one will promote to a queen.

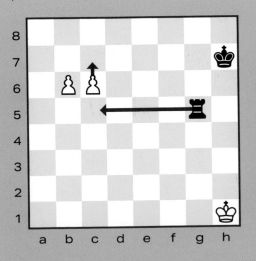

Safety moves

In your early games, you should play safely and look out for threats. The most obvious threat is that a piece will be captured but there are other tactical threats.

1 The white rook on **f6** is under attack from the king. It must run away but it is not safe to place it on any square marked with a red cross. The squares with the green tick are safe.

2

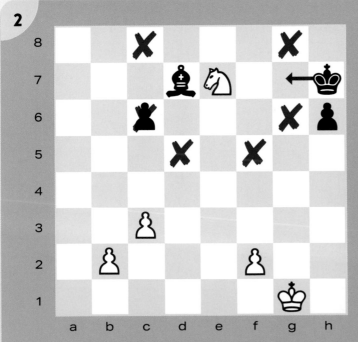

The white knight on **e7** has nowhere to go—it is said to be dominated by the bishop and king. The black king threatens to move across to **f7** and capture the knight.

White must do something to save the knight. We find the move **f4**. The f-pawn arrives at **f5** one move before the black king arrives at **f7**, giving the knight a safe square on **g6**. The f-pawn is lost but the knight is saved and there is a good chance that White will avoid losing.

Weak defenders

Even when you are protecting your pieces, you need to monitor whether the protection has been weakened, for example by a pin, a check, or a combination.

1   The black rook on **c4** seems to be protected by the **d5**-pawn. Black was surprised when the white queen captured the rook. Black had failed to notice that the **d5**-pawn is pinned against the black queen.

Black resigned because being a rook behind is too much to recover in a game between good players.

2   The black queen has captured a pawn on **d4** and appears to be protected by the knight on **c6**. However, the knight is not really defending because White can capture the knight with the bishop giving check to the black king. Black needs to respond to the check, for example by capturing the knight with the pawn. The white queen can then capture the black queen. White is a queen up and winning.

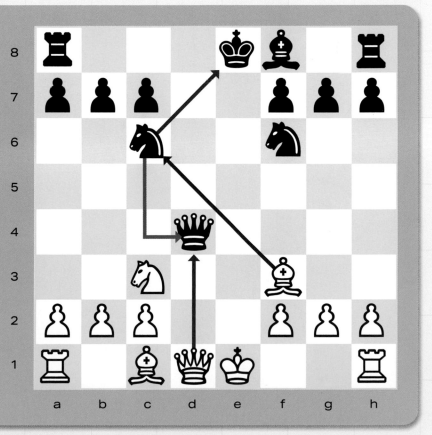

Counting before capturing a pawn

A successful attack usually requires more attackers than defenders, whether you're attacking a single pawn or a castled king.

1 Consider the black pawn at **d4**. It is being attacked by the white rook and behind that the white queen, a configuration known as a queen-rook battery. In short, there are two attackers. On the other side, there are two defenders, also a queen-rook battery. The number of defenders balances the number of attackers and the pawn is safe from being captured. If the white rook captures the pawn, it will be recaptured and unless White wants to lose the queen as well, the game is effectively over because Black is a rook ahead.

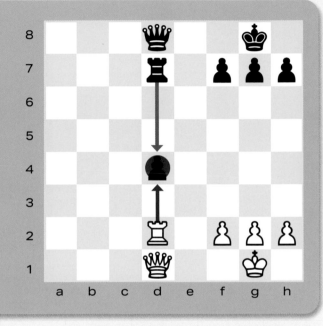

2

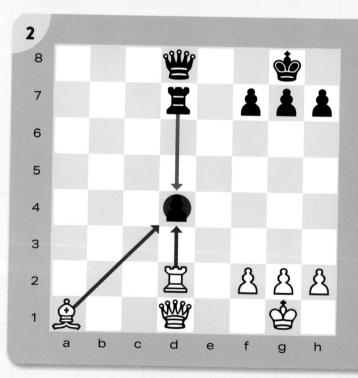

Suppose we add a bishop on **a1** pointing at the **d4**-pawn. There are now three pieces attacking the pawn and only two pieces defending. Now it is possible to capture the pawn. If the white rook captures the pawn, Black is forced to exchange the rooks because the black rook is pinned against its queen. After the rooks are exchanged the white queen on **d4** threatens the black queen and also checkmate on **g7** so the queens must be exchanged as well. White ends up a bishop ahead which is enough to win.

Defensive play

A lot of games are lost because players did not take sufficient precautions to protect against checkmate or a piece being lost. Here are some tricks to look out for.

1

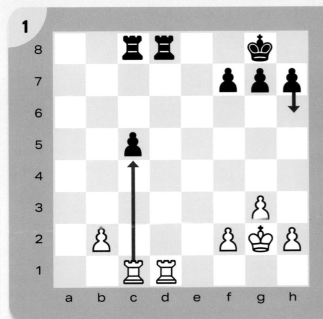

Avoid back rank checkmate

Back rank checkmate is common when beginners play.

You can avoid it by moving the h-pawn in front of the short-castled king.

Back rank checkmate is often a tactical factor. Here we see that White can capture the **c5** pawn with impunity by **Rxc5**. Black cannot then capture either white rook because the other white rook would deliver checkmate.

2 ## Beware in-between attacks on queen or king

The bishop on **g5** is no longer performing a useful role and should have retreated or captured the knight. Black plays **1...Nxe4** and if **2.Bxe7 Nxc3**! Black does not need to recapture the bishop on **e7** immediately because it has an in-between move which threatens to capture the queen with check and win a bishop. White's best response is **2.Qxe4**, only losing a pawn.

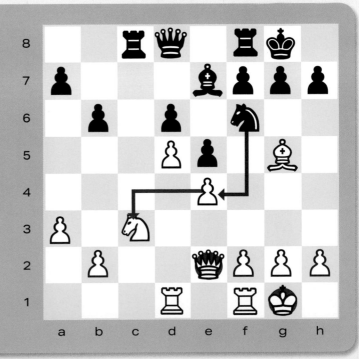

CHECK & CHECKMATE

You win a game of chess by checkmate. This means that there is no way to stop the king from being captured.

1   Here, the white king cannot move to any square marked in red, because these are under attack from the queen, pawns, and the black king.

So the only two squares that the white king can move to are **c4**, or to **c5** to capture the pawn.

2   The only squares that the white king can move to are **b4** and **d5**.

The king cannot move to **b3** because that square is attacked by the pawn on **a4**. It cannot move forward to **b5** or **c5** because the enemy king is there. It cannot go to **d3** because of the bishop on **f5**.

3   The black king is under attack from the rook. When a king is under attack, it is said to be "in check."

The king is not allowed to remain in check and so must move off the 8th rank. However, it cannot move to **c7** or **d7** because these are next to the opponent's king. So the only possible move is king to **b7**.

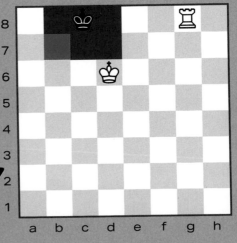

Giving check

Look out for ways to attack the king. When you give check, it is a forcing move—your opponent cannot ignore it. They have to respond to the check to get rid of the attack.

1 This shows how the king can be under attack from any of the pieces. We write a **+** sign when the king is in check. There are four checks possible here:

Ra4-a8+   **Be3-g5+**

Nd4-e6+   **c6-c7+**

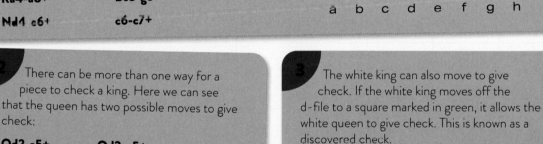

2 There can be more than one way for a piece to check a king. Here we can see that the queen has two possible moves to give check:

Qd2-a5+   **Qd2-g5+**

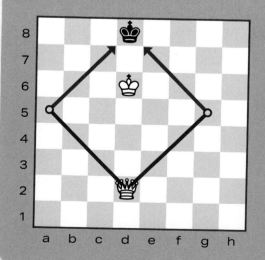

3 The white king can also move to give check. If the white king moves off the d-file to a square marked in green, it allows the white queen to give check. This is known as a discovered check.

Kd6-c6+   **Kd6-e6+**

Kd6-c5+   **Kd6-e6+**

Responding to Check

When you're in check, you'll need to find a way out.

The word "check" originally came from the game of chess! Originally, to 'put in check' meant to stop or control something. From this, "check" came to mean "make sure something is correct."

1 Kings are not allowed to remain in check. Black must do something about the check from the rook.

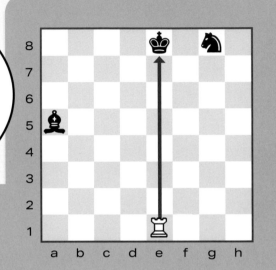

2 There are three ways to get out of check. Use this "ABC" to see if you can:

- Run **A**way—to one of the green squares

- **B**lock the attack with one of your pieces (**Ng8-e7**)

- **C**apture the attacking piece (**Ba5xRe1**)

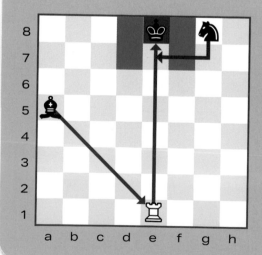

3 Here the black king is in check from the rook.

It cannot run away by moving to any of the squares marked with red because these are attacked by the opponent's king or rook. Black can't block the attack either.

White can get out of check by capturing the rook on **c8: Kd8xRc8**.

When the king is in check and has no way of getting out of it, it is in checkmate.

The player who gives checkmate is the winner.

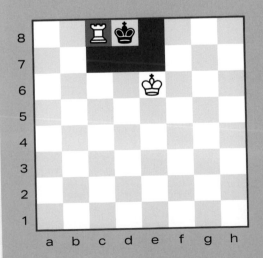

Rook checkmates

Checkmate by a rook is very common, especially in the endgame. Rooks often give checkmate on the edge of the board.

1 The king is in check from the rook. Unfortunately, the king cannot move forward because it is blocked by its own pawns. The king cannot run away because it would still be in check on **f8** or **h8**. There are no other black pieces to block the attack. Checkmate!

The checkmate shown is known as a back rank mate.

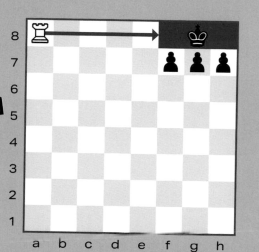

2 The black king is in check from the rook. Unfortunately, the king cannot move forward because it is blocked by the opposing king. The king cannot run away because it would still be in check on **c8** or **e8**. There are no other black pieces to block the attack. Black is in checkmate!

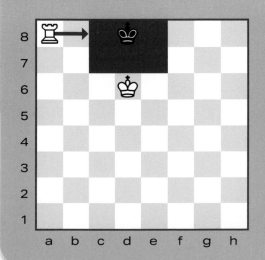

3 The black king is in check from the rook on **a1**. The king would still be under attack if it moved to another square on the 8th rank. Unfortunately, the king cannot move to the 7th rank because it would then be under attack by the other rook. There are no other black pieces to block the attack.

This checkmate is known as a lawnmower mate because the rooks combine together like lawnmower blades.

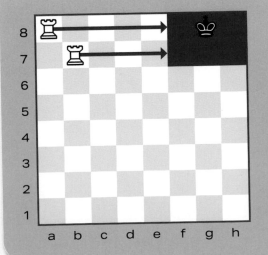

Queen checkmates

When the opponent's king is on the edge of the board, see if you can get your queen to stand next to it to deliver checkmate. The queen needs to be protected by one of its army.

1 The black king is in checkmate from the queen. The king has no safe square because the king and all the squares around the king are attacked by the queen. The king cannot capture the queen because it is protected by the pawn on **e6**.

2 The black king is in checkmate from the queen. As in the previous position, the king is in check and has nowhere safe to go. The queen is protected by the bishop.

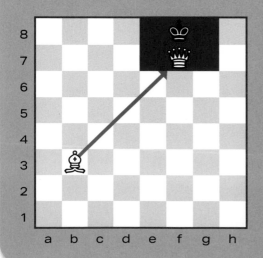

3 Pieces can combine to attack the squares around the king. Here we see that the queen delivers checkmate on **f6** protected by the knight. The king cannot retreat to the 8th rank because that is under attack from the rook.

Queen checkmate patterns

Some queen checkmate patterns are so well known that they have been given names, usually after the first person to describe them or play them in a game. We're showing these patterns without the white king, because it is not involved.

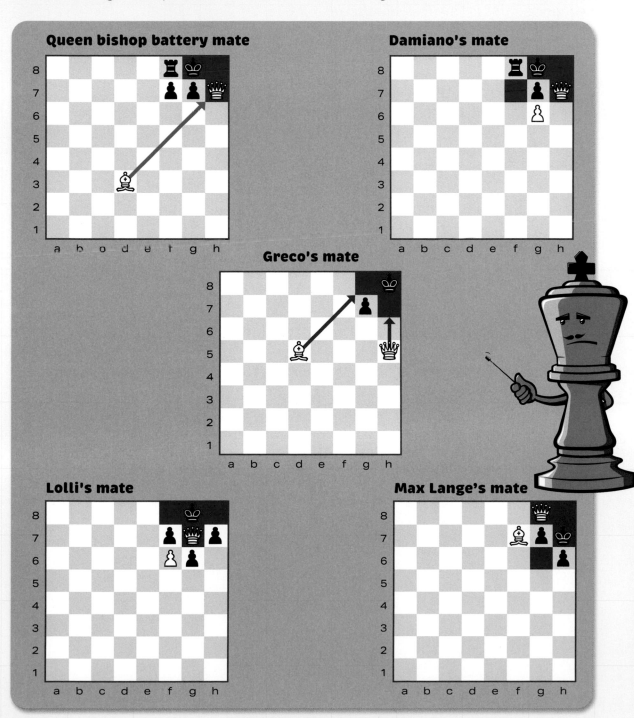

Queen bishop battery mate

Damiano's mate

Greco's mate

Lolli's mate

Max Lange's mate

Smothered mate

A special type of checkmate is when the king is surrounded by pieces at the edge of the board. The knight attacks the king at the end of a forcing sequence—this is called a "smothered mate."

1 This is the typical configuration for smothered mate. The queen has put the king in check. Blocking the attack with the rook fails because the queen, supported by the knight, can capture the rook.

2 If the king moves into the corner then the knight will deliver check from **f7**. Unless Black gives up the rook for the knight, the king must move back to **g8**. The stage is set for the key move.

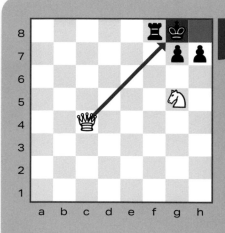

3 The knight retreats to **h6** to create a double check—the discovered check from the queen and the check from the knight. The only move for the king is back into the corner. The stage is set for the finale.

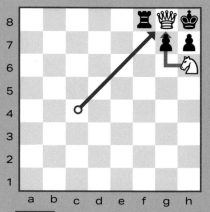

4 The queen gives check on **g8**. The king cannot capture the queen because it is protected by the knight. So the rook must capture the queen.

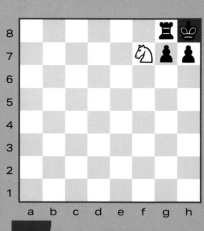

5 Finally, the knight delivers smothered checkmate on **h8**.

Other checkmate patterns

There are so many ways to give checkmate. Here are some more...

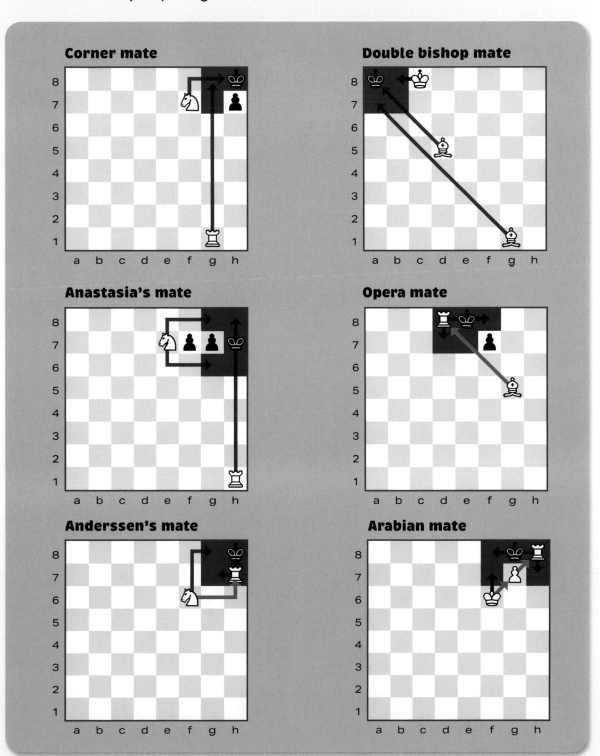

Corner mate

Double bishop mate

Anastasia's mate

Opera mate

Anderssen's mate

Arabian mate

OPENINGS

With so many ways to start a game, it's good to have some basic guidelines on how to begin.

Control the center

Try to occupy the center with your pawns and knights, and prevent your opponent from doing the same.

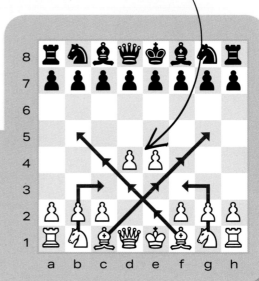

Try to keep one pawn in the center

1 The moves **1.e4** and **1.d4** not only control the center but also open up space for you to get your bishops out quickly. Develop knights before bishops because the knights have fewer squares at the outset and hence you keep your options open with the bishops. Beginners make the mistake of moving **1.a4** and **1.h4** to let out the rooks, but they do not belong on the flanks.

2 Let's take a look at the Italian Opening.

White plays **5.Nbd2** which moves the knight toward the center. However, this blocks the development of the bishop at **c1** and removes a useful square for the queen at **d2**. It is not a mistake, but inaccuracies tend to accumulate until you realize you do not like your position.

A more flexible move would be **5.Nc3**.

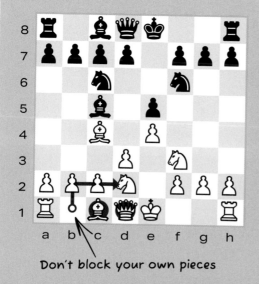

Don't block your own pieces

3 White has developed the knights and bishops to active squares where they are pointing at the center. White's last move **6.Bg5** pins the knight on **f6**. This is indirectly controlling the center because White threatens to play **Nd5** bringing more pressure on **Nf6** and potentially wrecking the kingside pawns by exchanging on **f6** because the black queen cannot recapture.

Avoid moving your knights to the edge of the board because they have less mobility there, unless there is a specific purpose.

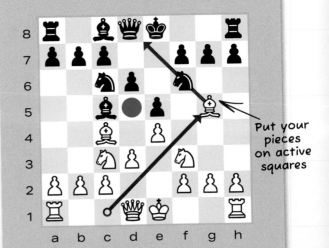

Put your pieces on active squares

Develop your pieces

"Developing" your pieces means to move them from their starting square to a more effective square. The power of your army greatly increases if the pieces can combine harmoniously with each other. Each of the pieces needs to find a square where it can exert its powers.

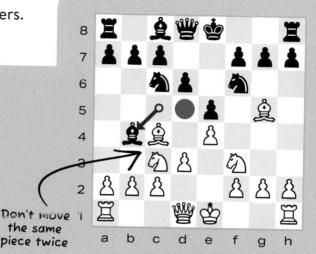

4 Moving a piece twice is a waste of time if you could have moved there in one move. Here Black wants to stop White playing **Nd5** by playing **6...Bb4**. The idea is plausible and the move isn't a blunder, but it is an admission that the king's bishop was not on the correct square.

The most common way to deal with a pin is **6...h6** which pushes the bishop away before White can play **7. Nd5**.

Don't move the same piece twice

5 The white queen is part of a queen-bishop battery attacking the **h7** pawn which is protected by the knight on **f6**. Even if that knight is captured by the bishop on **g5**, the other knight can recapture thus restoring the defense. Meanwhile both sides target **e4**.

The queen starts with a small step

Advanced Tip

The queen is the most powerful piece, but don't move it more than one or two squares for its first move. If the queen is in front of its pawns, then it will be vulnerable to attack.

Time in chess is measured as one tempo per move. So moving a piece twice is a waste of a tempo.

King safety

Always put your king safely in the corner by castling. Develop your pieces and castle your king before you consider what to do next. Here are some common king pawn openings, up to the point of castling by White.

1   Italian Game

1.e4 e5 2.Nf3 Nc6 3.Bc4 Bc5 4. 0-0

2   Spanish Opening

1.e4 e5 2.Nf3 Nc6 3.Bb5 a6 4.Ba4 Nf6 5.0-0

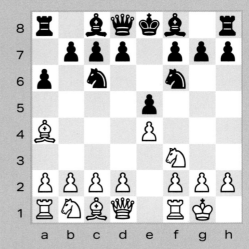

3   French Defense, Advance Variation

1.e4 e6 2.d4 d5 3.e5 c5 4.c3 Nc6 5.Nf3 Qb6 6.a3 c4 7.Nbd2 Na5 8.Be2 Bd7 9.0-0

4   Caro Kann Defense, Advance Variation

1.e4 c6 2.d4 d5 3.e5 Bf5 4.Bd3 Bxd3 5.Qxd3 e6 6.Nf3 Qb6 7.0-0

Keep pawns close to the king

The king is only safe if the pawns in front of it are undisturbed. If a pawn in front of the castled king has moved, then it can be the target of attack.

1 Robert J. Fischer (USA) vs. Bent Larsen (Denmark) Portoroz, 1958

Black castled first and then White castled on the opposite side. Fischer advanced the h-pawn to open up an attack on the castled king. The target is the pawn on **g6**. There was a good reason for putting the pawn on **g6**—to fianchetto the bishop on **g7**—but this formation is vulnerable to an assault by "Harry the h-pawn." Larsen resigned 13 moves later.

2 Levon Aronian (Armenia) vs. Vladimir Kramnik (Russia), Berlin, 2018

White castled and then weakened the defenses around the king by playing **h3**. Black, a former World Champion, targeted the **h3** pawn by advancing the g-pawn supported by a rook and won eventually.

Opening as White

Every player needs to develop a set of moves as White and as Black. As White, you make the first move and can choose the opening. For a beginner, it is best to use an opening system which you can play no matter what your opponent does, at least for the first few moves. One effective set of moves is known as the London System, which was popularized a century ago at a tournament in London.

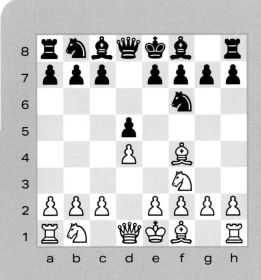

1 The opening moves of the London System

The queen's bishop gets to **f4** quickly so that it is outside the pawn chain when White plays **e3** to support the central pawn at **d4**.

2 These moves result in a solid configuration of pieces. White has focused on developing the pieces and getting the king into safety.

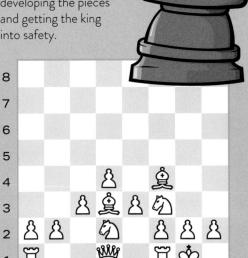

3 A few moves later, the rooks are centralized and there is a knight on **e5**. The precise moves by White will depend upon what Black does.

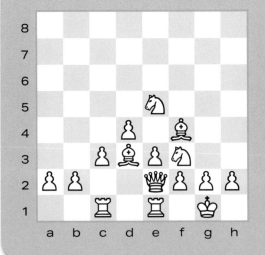

Using the London System

To see the London System in action, let's look at a game between Vladimir Kramnik (Russia), a former world chess champion and Hou Yifan (China), the highest-rated female player ever.

1 This is the position after 11 moves. You can see that White has followed the basic pattern of the London System. The opening moves are done, and we're entering the middle game.

2 **12.Bxd6 Qxd6 13.Ne5 Rad8 14.Qf3 Ng6 15.Bxg6 hxg6 16.Qh3 Ba6 17.Rfe1 Nh7 18.f4 Bb5 19.Ndf3 Qe7 20.Qg3**

White has a well-placed knight on **e5** supported by two pawns and the other knight.

3 **20. Be8 21.Rf1 Qf6**

Putting the black queen at the front of the defense on the kingside is a mistake. It is too valuable to exchange with any of the white pieces.

4 **22.Ng5 Qe7 23.Rf3**

Black retreats the queen and White uses the time gained to advance the knight and the rook via **f3**, putting more pressure on Black. White went on to win the game.

Defending as Black

Did you know that players of the white pieces have a slightly better chance of winning? This is because White has the advantage of choosing the opening. Black must find a way of responding.

The same systematic approach can be used in defense as well as in attack. You can play the same move 1...c6 in response to any opening and obtain a solid position in which you can develop your pieces easily.

If your opponent opens with the king's pawn, it's the **Caro Kann Defense.**

If your opponent opens with the queen's pawn, it's the **Slav Defense.**

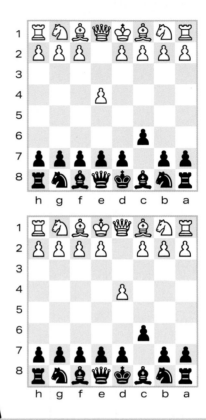

The Caro Kann Defense

1   1.e4 c6 2.d4 d5 3.Nc3

Black plays **2...d5** to challenge White's pawn at **e4**. White defends the pawn on **e4** with the knight on **c3**. This is the Classical Variation.

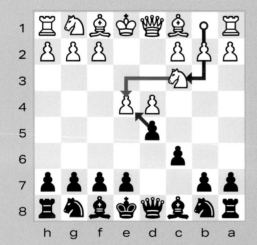

2   3...dxe4 4.Nxe4 Bf5 5.Ng3 Bg6

Black exchanges the central pawns and has an easy development. If White now plays **6.h4** to attack the bishop on **g6**, Black will create a retreat square by **6...h7**.

The Slav Defense

1 The white pawn on **c4** is under attack and not defended. This is known as the Queen's Gambit. A gambit refers to giving up a pawn for some compensation, such as more space or a strong center.

2 **1.d4 c6 2.c4 d5 3.Nf3 Nf6 4.Nc3 dxc4**

The **c4** can now be taken. If White moves the king's pawn to let out the bishop **5.e3** or **5.e4**, then Black can support its extra pawn with **5... b5** and White cannot get the **c4** pawn back immediately.

Therefore, White should play **5.a4**, but this gives time for Black to develop its queen's bishop to **f5**.

3 **5.a4 Bf5 6.e3 e6 7.Bxc4 Bd6**

Black can develop easily with **Nbd7**, **0-0**, **Qe7** and, at some point, the equalizing move **c6-c5**.

Players spend more time studying openings than any other stage of the game. However, you only need to know the first few moves of an opening. After that, you should follow the general advice: control the center, develop your pieces, ensure king safety, and find good squares for your pieces.

STRATEGY

Once you have developed your pieces and castled your king, you need to find a plan.

The plan needs to be flexible so that you can change it depending upon the position. A plan needs to be practical and refer to specific moves or patterns. Keep revising your strategy as you go!

1 Black is a pawn down, so wants to avoid any exchanges. After **1.Rd2+** the black king cannot go to the e-file because of **1.Re2+** forcing the exchange of rooks. So Black moves to the c-file.

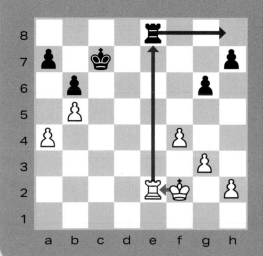

2 White now plays **2.Re2** challenging the black rook which must avoid the exchange. Wherever it goes, White will play **3.Re7+**.

Merely the threat of exchanges is enough to improve the position of the person with material advantage.

3 Black is determined not to exchange any material with the result that the black pieces have become completely passive. White's plan is create a passed pawn on **f5** and/or to infiltrate Black's kingside pawns.

Material advantage

When you have gained material advantage then review your strategy. Even just being a pawn ahead is enough to win the game if you can reach the endgame and promote that extra pawn into a queen. If you are material ahead, then you should exchange pieces. The less the material on the board, the more your material advantage will count.

How to use tactics

"Tactics flow from a superior position." This is a famous quotation from the great American grandmaster Bobby Fischer. The first part of the game is when you develop your pieces, put your king in safety, and slowly improve your position by accumulating small positional advantages. The improvements you can make include the following...

Open up lines

When you are ahead in development, open up lines. Your opponent may waste time in the opening by grabbing a pawn or moving the same piece twice. Exchange pawns to open the files and diagonals for your better coordinated pieces.

Swap off your opponent's well-placed pieces

If an opponent's piece is controlling vital squares in your position, challenge it with your own piece. For example, if they have a knight on **e5**, put your knight on **d7**.

Put pressure on opponent's weak points

If your opponent has a backward pawn, you can bear down on that pawn with your pieces. When your opponent defends, you can switch to attacking another point.

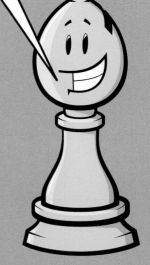

"Tactics" is when you look ahead two or three moves. "Strategy" is when you look ahead several moves more.

Improving your position

Once each piece has been developed, they always need to find better squares. Always be alert for a chance to gain material through a tactic—and look out for the tactics of your opponent. Here are some rules of thumb to improve your position, providing the chosen move is safe. Of course, if these ideas benefit you they also benefit your opponent, so you should aim to stop your opponent from using them!

Rooks

- Put your rook opposite the enemy queen or king
- Make sure no piece blocks the connection between the rooks
- Put rooks on open files
- Get a rook to the 7th rank (or 2nd rank if you are playing black) if safe
- Double rooks to put pressure on a file or backward pawn

Knights

- Put knights on central outposts protected by a pawn
- Seek to exchange any well-placed knights of the opponent
- Knights are better than bishops in blocked positions
- "Knights on the rim are dim"! Get the knight back into the game

Bishops

- Put your bishop on the same diagonal as the enemy queen or king
- Try to keep both bishops, because they work well together

Queen

- The queen is needed most when you have decided to attack the king
- The queen makes a poor defender
- The queen works better with the knight than a bishop in attack
- If you have only one bishop, put the queen on the opposite color

Pawns

- Try to keep at least one pawn in the center. Pawns should capture toward the center.
- Pawns should support each other in pawn chains.
- Keep pawns side by side, because then either pawn can break forward.
- Do not advance a pawn beyond the 5th rank, because it becomes difficult to defend.
- Avoid these pawn weaknesses:
    - Doubled pawns (two pawns on the same file)
    - Backward pawns (a pawn which cannot be supported by its colleagues)
    - Isolated pawns (no supporting pawns) unless on **d4** supporting a knight
- Apart from a standard opening gambit (e.g. Queen's Gambit) do not sacrifice a pawn unless you obtain one of these benefits:
    - It prevents the opponent from castling
    - It develops an attack
    - It reflects the opponent's queen from the center (a "poisoned pawn")
    - It gains two tempi (moves) or more—see page 65 for more about tempo

Pawn formations

Deploy your footsoldiers to create weaknesses in the opponent's position, or to create a passed pawn: one that has no opponent pawns in its way.

Minority Attack

1

In queen pawn openings, the c-pawn often gets exchanged for the e-pawn. The resulting pawn formation is known as the Carlsbad formation.

The Minority Attack refers to White advancing the a and b pawns to exchange against their opposite numbers to leave a pawn at **c6** which can then be attacked by rooks doubled on the c-file and a knight on **e5**.

2 **Sammy Reshevsky (USA) vs. Lhamsuren Myagmarsuren (Mongolia), 1967**

In this game, Reshevsky played **b5**, putting pressure on the **c6** pawn.

3

25.b5 Qd7 26.bxc6 Rxc6 27.Qb5 Rec8 28.Rbc1 R8c7 29.g4 a6 30.Qxa6 Nf6 31.Nxd5!

Black has gathered its pieces to defend the c-pawn. White plays the excellent move **31.Nxd5!**

4 **Nxd5 32.Rxc6 Rxc6 33.Qa8+ 1-0**

Black deals with the knight fork threat and White exchanges rooks on **c6**. Black had overlooked that White had three attackers against **c6** because the white queen can give check on **a8** which forks the king and rook on **c6**. White is the exchange and two pawns ahead, so Black resigned.

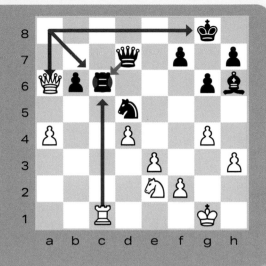

Stonewall Attack

1 The Stonewall formation is characterized by a solid group of pawns on **c3**, **d4**, **e3**, and **f4**. It is designed for attacking the black king. It supports an outpost on **e5** for a knight and a diagonal toward **h7** on for a bishop or queen both. The formation will withstand pawn exchanges because the **c3** and **e3** pawns are protectors.

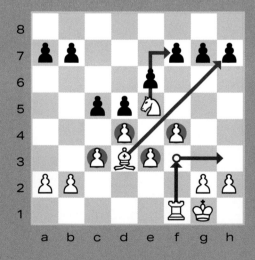

2 **Yaacov Norowitz vs. Vlad Ionut Stegariu, internet, 2020**

Black blocks the threat of checkmate on **h7** by interposing the f-pawn. White launches a vigorous attack, starting with **g4**.

Attacking the King

You need to learn how to attack the king if you want to make progress in chess. The king is usually well defended so it is not an easy task. It is exciting to attack the king, but don't do it unless the conditions are right.

Ideally you should prevent your opponent from castling. You may be able do this by making the king move to avoid a check or recapture a piece, or by attacking a square which the king must pass over.

Attack or defend?

You should usually have more attacking pieces than defending pieces. Sometimes the opponent will have their pieces on the queenside of the board, neglecting the king. Or you may be able to decoy, deflect, or block their defending pieces.

Three coordinated pieces can create a checkmate

A knight on an advanced outpost often plays a vital role. The queen and knight often weave a mating net. A queen supported by a bishop can be launched at the king. A rook can cut off the king's escape squares. The rook can also swing horizontally to join the fray.

Here are some techniques for attacking kingside formations...

Scholar's Mate

1.e4 e5 2.Qh5 Nc6 3.Bf4 Nf6? 4. Qxf7#

This quick checkmate is quite common among beginners. White relies upon Black not having a clue about what is happening. The queen and white-squared bishop combine to deliver checkmate on **f7**. The scholar's mate is easy to parry, for example Black could play **3...g6** pushing the queen away.

Queen Bishop Battery

White's queen and bishop are looking at **h7** and White threatens **1.Bxf6** to capture the protective knight, followed by the queen capturing **h7** with check and checkmate to follow. Black must defend by **1...g6** to create a bulwark against the queen-bishop battery. However, this weakens the kingside and White will now focus on breaking into the kingside in another way, for example by **2.Qf2** aiming for **h4**.

Greek Gift Sacrifice

The black king has castled but its defensive knight at **f6** has been driven away by the pawn at **e5** and it is vulnerable to attack on **h7**. The classic sacrifice of the light-squared bishop on **h7** is known as the Greek Gift, an allusion to the mythical wooden horse the Greeks gave to the Trojans which hid some soldiers. Taking the bishop at **h7** leads to a difficult game for Black because the white knight and queen are soon on the scene.

1.Bxh7+ Kxh7 2. Ng5+ Kg6 (best) 3. Qg4 f5 4. Qg3 Qe7 5. Nxe6+ Kh6 6.Nxf8 and White is winning.

Pawn Storm

The pawn storm is a direct threat to the castled king. White has taken the precaution of castling on the queenside so that the advancing pawns do not expose the white king. The pawns will cause havoc to the king's defenses or, if captured, will open up lines against the king.

Here the **g4** pawn is en prise which puts Black in a dilemma. If **1...Nxg4** then White can play **2. Qg2** followed by **3.Rg1** switching the attack to the g-file. If Black does not take the **g4** pawn then White can use it as a battering ram against the **h6** pawn.

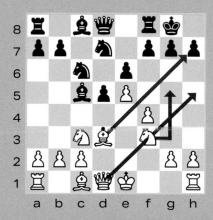

The Fianchettoed King

If the king is in a fianchetto formation, a standard attacking plan is to advance the h-pawn supported by a rook in order to prise open the kingside defences. Here we see Carissa Yip as White attacking her opponent in this way during an online tournament. Opposite side castling means that Black will also be trying to attack the white king—but only if they get a chance. In this game, White went on to win brilliantly.

ENDGAMES

An extra pawn in the endgame can be enough to win if it can be promoted to a queen. The difference between obtaining a win or a draw can depend upon whose move it is...

Center pawns

A pawn in the center of the board can decide the endgame.

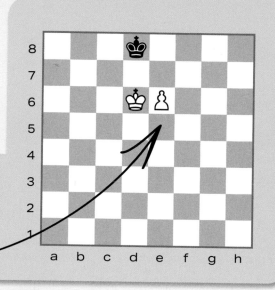

1 In this fundamental position, if it is White's turn, the game is drawn: **1. e7+ Ke8 2. Ke6** stalemate. If it is Black to move, White wins: **1... Ke8 2. e7 Kf7 3. Kd7** and the pawn promotes.

White to play: draw. Black to play: white wins

2 The key defensive idea is to occupy the square directly in front of the passed pawn. If it is Black to play, the only move is to retreat the king to **e8**. If White advances the king to **e6**, then we are back to the previous position which draws. The same defense applies symmetrically if White advanced to **f6**.

Draw

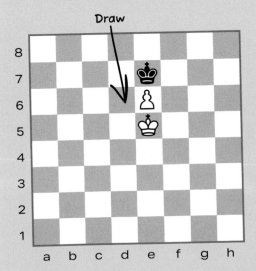

3 Always try to get your king in front of your passed pawn. For example, if **1. Kd6 Kd8 2. e6** and White wins.

White wins

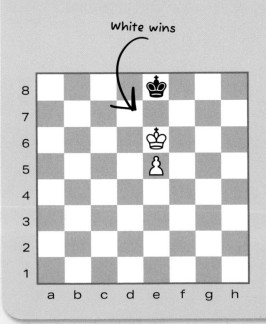

Activate the king

In king and pawn endgames, the king should be active and in front of its pawns.

White wins by activating the king.

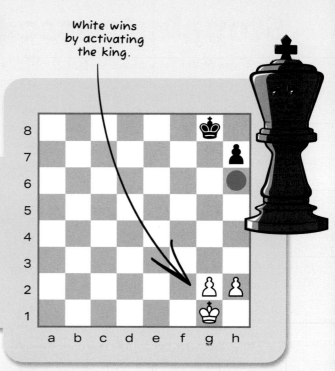

1 The best plan is to (a) advance the white king to the critical square **h6** (marked) which ties down the black king to the defense of the pawn, which to defend the pawn must move between **g8** and **h8**; (b) advance the pawns and create a passed pawn at **g6** when the black king is at **h8**. White wins. If Black moves the **h7** pawn, the white king will move alongside it and capture it.

2 The rook pawn is racing to **h8**. If the white king occupies the critical square **g7** (marked), it can prevent the black king from getting near the pawn. However, if Black can prevent White from getting to **g7** then Black will be able to stop the pawn either by occupying the corner **h8** or else by occupying the f file and forcing the white king to remain in front of its pawn.

Whoever has the move will achieve their objective: a win for White or a draw for Black.

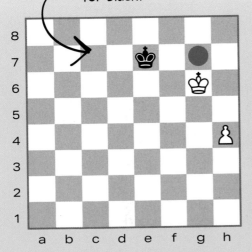

3 White cannot win because if its king retreats to **h5**, Black will gain the **g7** square. However, if the white king advances to **h7**, Black will follow to **f7** and will mirror White's move each time.

Draw because the white king is pressed against the edge

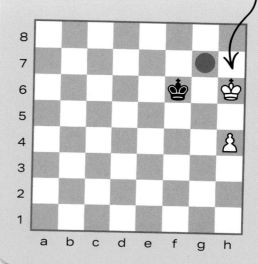

81

Stopping passed pawns

A passed pawn is a pawn with no opponent's pawns in front of it—ready to reach the end of the board and promote. The king is typically involved in creating or guarding passed pawns.

1 White is a pawn ahead and can win with a simple plan. Advance the h-pawn and the black king must stop it. When the black king moves toward the pawn, it will abandon the **e5** square which the white king will occupy. White will then capture the **d5** pawn, put its king on **e6**, and escort its **d4** pawn to its destination.

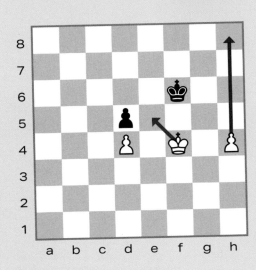

2 When the position is blocked, neither side can make progress. Any pawn which moves will be captured, for example **1.d6 Kxd6**. Black cannot capture the pawn on **e4** because it needs to guard the protected passed pawn on **d5**. So the kings will shuffle backward and forward—a draw.

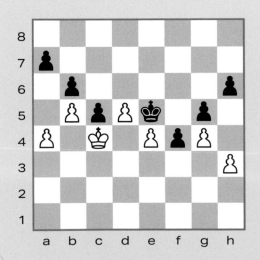

3 In the previous position, if Black tried **1...f3** the white king on **c4** has it covered. The pawn takes three moves to reach the end—the same number of moves as the king. The "queening box" marks the area where the king must be placed if it is to catch a passed pawn in the box.

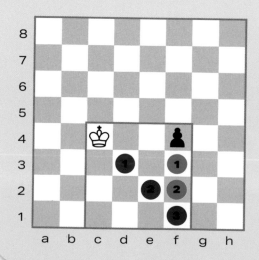

Outside passed pawn

When you create an outside passed pawn—one that is far from the kings—it diverts the opponent's king, allowing you to create a second passed pawn on the other side of the board.

1 White has a pawn majority on the kingside and can create a passed pawn with **g5**. For example, **1.g5 hxg5+ 2. Kxg5** and the h-pawn will reach the end. The problem for Black is that the **c6** pawn is "backward"—it cannot be supported by other pawns and will be captured if it moves forward. Black cannot create a passed pawn without giving White another passed pawn on **c5**. The game could continue **2...c5 3. dxc5 d4** bringing us to the next position.

2 Black is threatening to promote the d-pawn. White may be tempted to go for a pawn race with **4.c6**, but this would be a mistake because the black king can stop the c-pawn by **Kd7** at the right moment whereas the white king cannot stop the d-pawn after **4...d3**. The correct move in this position for White is **4. Kf4** which brings the king into the queening box.

3 We see that Black's d-pawn has been neutralized. Meanwhile, Black cannot stop both the c-pawn and the h-pawn. Whichever pawn the black king approaches, the other pawn will run.

Thinking ahead

In the endgame, you need to calculate ahead further than in other parts of the game. Many calculations are about king safety and passed pawns.

1 White is behind in material by the exchange **(RvN)** and three pawns. The white king is very active and sees a chance by moving to **f8**—the king and knight are combining with the threat of **Nf7** checkmate.

The rook would like to give check on **f3** and force the white king back. However, the **f3** square is covered by the knight. Black does not want to give up the rook so easily.

2 So Black has another idea and advances the rook pawn to **h5**. This move has two purposes—to give some "luft" (which means "air" in German) to the king which is stuck in the corner, and to run to the other side of the board to promote. This seems dangerous for White because the h-pawn only needs four moves to reach the end and it does not look like the knight can stop it.

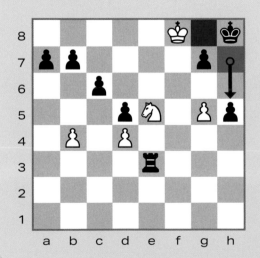

3 White can see that the h-pawn is running but persists in the strategy of trying to get checkmate first. White ignores the h-pawn and advances the pawn to **g6** which completely blocks the black king.

Now **Nf7** checkmate is threatened again.

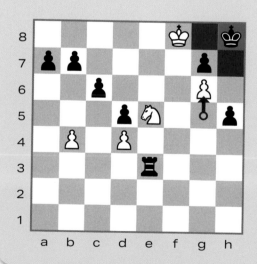

4 White has no choice but to capture the knight to avoid immediate checkmate. We now have a pawn race. Black plays **h4** and both players will reach the opposite side in three moves.

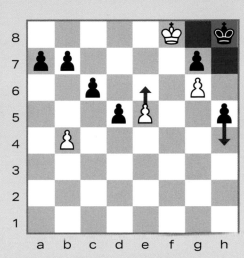

5 White's d-pawn promotes immediately prior to black's h-pawn.

This would all have been calculated from the original position.

White now has a rare experience—giving checkmate by moving the king.

6 The white king moves to **f7**, opening the way for the queen to give checkmate. This discovered checkmate came at the end of the long sequence, but one in which nearly all the moves were forced.

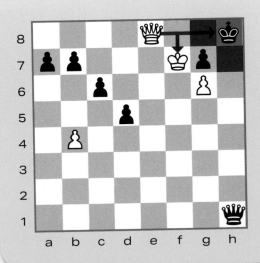

Rook & pawn endings

Half of the games in chess reduce to rook endings, so it is important to understand some basics.

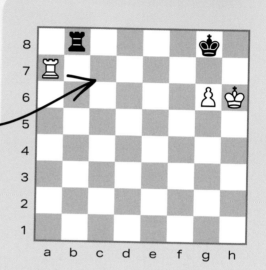

Black can defend this position

1 White is a single pawn ahead, but can't promote the pawn if Black keeps the rook on the back rank to defend against checkmate. If White advances its pawn, then the black rook will check the white king from the b-file. The only way to escape these checks is to come over to the queenside, but this leaves the pawn unprotected.

2 Having a passed pawn further toward the center makes this into a winning position for White. The difference is that the white rook can get to the h-file. For example, **1.Rg7+ Kh8 2. Rh7+ Kg7 3. f7+ Kf8 4. Rh8+** and White has skewered the king and rook.

White can win this position

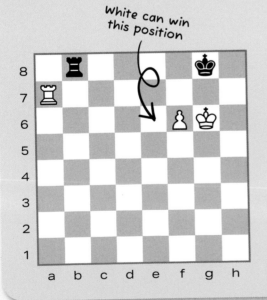

3 If the white king is on the same side of the pawn as the black rook, then Black has more opportunities to give check from the side. If the white king tries to escape the checks by getting to the other side of the pawn, then Black is no longer under the immediate threat of checkmate and has a chance to start checking from the far side **1.Kf5 Rb1 2. Kg6 Rg1+**. The king cannot shake off the checks.

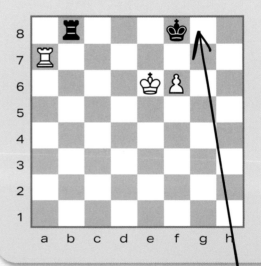

Black must be active to defend this position

Endgame tactics

Even when the number of pieces is reduced, there are still tricks in the endgame to look out for.

1 Being a queen down is almost always lost. An exception is if you have a passed rook or bishop pawn. Here, if the queen captures the bishop pawn, black is in stalemate.

Being a queen ahead does not always win

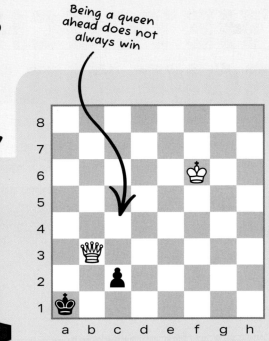

2 At first it looks like Black is winning with the outside passed h-pawn. However, after **1.b6 cxb6 2. a6** White breaks through and promotes one of its pawns by sacrificing two pawns. Meanwhile, White is within the queening square of the **h4** pawn preventing it from promotion.

White to play can break through and get a queen.

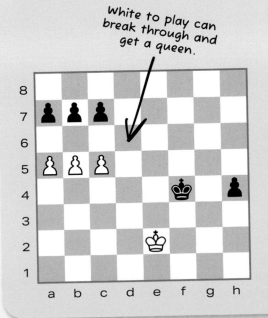

3 The skewer tactic can be particularly effective when a rook supports pawn promotion.

Sometimes a rook supports the advance of a passed pawn to the seventh rank from the front. If the white rook leaves **a8** then the black rook will capture the **a7** pawn. However, White can succeed in another way. **1.Rh8 Rxa7 2. Rh7+** and the black king is skewered against the **a7** rook.

Look out for rook skewers on an open board

THE TOUCH MOVE RULE

Having the option to change your mind is not allowed in chess. When you play chess, you need to be decisive. Think about your move, weigh up the options, make a decision, and play the move. After that, you can't change your mind. As in life, you must live with the consequences of your actions.

> You can center a piece on a square without breaching the touch move rule. Before you touch the piece, just say "I adjust."

The touch move rule in chess has three elements:

1) If you touch a piece you must move it, if it's legal.

2) If you touch an opponent's piece, you must capture it, if possible.

3) Once you have lifted your finger off the piece, the move is complete.

The touch move rule applies to all competitive games of chess and is strictly enforced unless the touching was clearly accidental.

There can be disputes if one person says a piece was touched and the other person denies it. If this happens, then the tournament controller must determine the course of action to follow.

You need to make sure than when you castle, you move the king first and the rook second. You are not allowed to move both pieces at the same time.

Some beginners have a habit of thinking by touching. The solution is "Sit on your hands!" After a while, you'll be able to think in your head. Another trick for beginners is to keep your finger on the piece for a bit longer and check that the square is safe. Sometimes you need to place a piece on a square to be able to see what attacks it. Don't do this too often, because you block your opponent from seeing a part of the board, and they could complain.

USING A CHESS CLOCK

There was a time that chess players took as long as they liked to make a move. Players would even fall asleep waiting for their opponent to move! This changed in 1851 with the arrival of the chess clock at the first international chess tournament in London.

In tournaments, your move is not complete until you press the clock. You must use the same hand to press the clock as move the piece.

You have a certain amount of time to play. If you did not play all your moves within the time limit, then you lose. This can make some players make blunders in the rush of making moves quickly.

In the USA, the system used is known as time delay. The clock pauses for 5 seconds of every turn before counting down. Domestic USA events are usually very time-limited, so increments are avoided except at the top level.

Other countries use incremental time. This means that each player gets a fixed amount of time at the start of the game, and then up to 30 seconds is added per move. This extra time means that players can think about their moves during the endgame. With time increments, players can add time to their clocks if they move fast enough, which is not possible with time delay.

For all major International Chess Federation events, at classical time controls, 90 minutes is given to both players for 40 moves, after which the players get an extra 30 minutes to complete the entire game. 30 seconds per move is added from the beginning.

Top time tips

When using a clock, try to allocate time evenly throughout the game. Beginners often panic when they use a clock and play out the moves quickly not allowing enough thinking time. Some players have a tendency to think for too long in the opening and middlegame and then run out of time.

Try to have more time left than your opponent. When you reach a crucial position and a big decision is required, you will need to spend more time. If a move is forced or obvious then make it quickly.

Advanced Tip

If your opponent breaks a rule, e.g. makes an illegal move, stop the clock and call the arbiter or tournament controller. The penalty imposed may be to add two minutes extra to your clock.

CHESS TOURNAMENTS

Chess tournaments can be very exciting, as people from near and far gather to play. The way to prove yourself in the chess world is to do well in a tournament. There are two main formats: Swiss System and All Play All. The scoring is one point for a win, half a point for a draw, and no points for a loss.

Swiss System

In the Swiss System, in each round you are paired against someone with a similar number of points as yourself. You do not know who you will be playing until just before the round.

Ladder

If you want to run a competition over a whole season, you can use a ladder format. This is a list of players which is ordered according to their performance. A player lower down the list can challenge someone higher up. If the challenger wins, they move up the ladder to replace their opponent who drops down one place. If the challenger loses, there is no change to the positions.

All Play All

When the number of participants is limited, each of the participants plays each of the others. All Play All events are regarded as the fairest way to find out the best player in a group. It is also a way to see how famous players perform against each other.

Quads

In schools and clubs, sometimes events are organized in groups of four players. Each player plays the other players in the group, so there are three games each.

Chess ratings

If you start playing in a chess tournament you will earn an "Elo rating," named after the professor who invented it. As you win games, your rating goes up, and as you lose games your rating goes down. If you beat a stronger player, your rating goes up more than if you beat a weaker player. Many sports and games have adopted the Elo system, including football, basketball, and baseball.

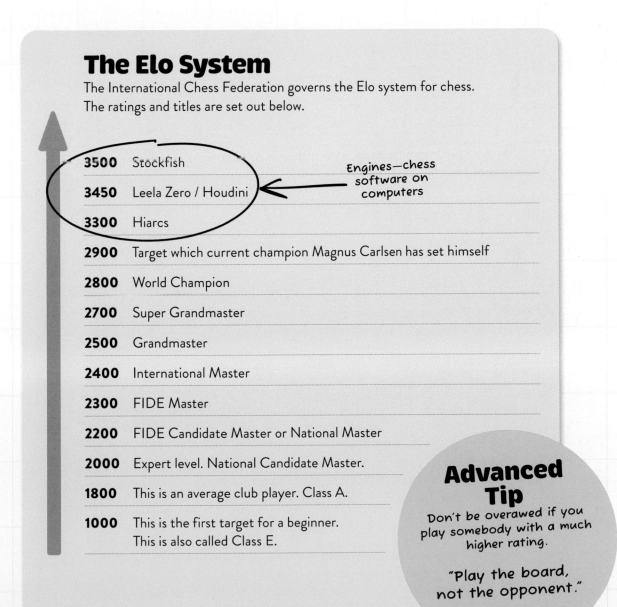

The Elo System

The International Chess Federation governs the Elo system for chess. The ratings and titles are set out below.

3500	Stockfish
3450	Leela Zero / Houdini
3300	Hiarcs
2900	Target which current champion Magnus Carlsen has set himself
2800	World Champion
2700	Super Grandmaster
2500	Grandmaster
2400	International Master
2300	FIDE Master
2200	FIDE Candidate Master or National Master
2000	Expert level. National Candidate Master.
1800	This is an average club player. Class A.
1000	This is the first target for a beginner. This is also called Class E.

Engines—chess software on computers

Advanced Tip

Don't be overawed if you play somebody with a much higher rating.

"Play the board, not the opponent."

How chess games end

A chess game ends if one of the following situations arises whether a win/lose or a draw:

Winning and losing

Checkmate. Although this is the most famous final move in chess, it is relatively rare because before that the player with an inferior position resigns the game.

Resignation is when a player decides that there is no point in playing any more because they are going to lose. The conventional way of showing this is to turn the king onto its side. The losing player extends their hand to congratulate their opponent.

Lose on time is when you have run out of the time allocated to play your game. This often arises in complicated positions and can be very annoying, but you can learn to manage your time better.

Disqualification is the penalty for committing a serious offense such as cheating by using a computer to analyze your moves.

Draws

When you score a draw you share the points with your opponent, typically half a point each.

Stalemate is when the player having the move is unable to make a legal move. It is an automatic draw. Stalemates arise in the endgame, especially when the king's movement is restricted.

Draw by mutual agreement. About one-third of chess games end in an agreed draw, usually because the position is level or chances are even.

Draw by threefold repetition. If you and your opponent reach the same position three times with the same person to move, you may claim a draw from your opponent or from the arbiter. If you fail to make the claim, and the same position is reached five times, then the draw is automatic.

Draw under the 50-move rule. If 50 moves have been played by each player without a pawn move or a capture, then you may claim a draw. If you fail to make the claim, and 75 moves have been played by each player without a pawn move or a capture, then the draw is automatic.

Draw due to a dead position. This may arise when the position is completely blocked. The most common reason is that there is insufficient material for either player to checkmate the opponent's king. Examples of insufficient material include:

- King vs. king
- King and minor piece (knight or bishop) vs. king
- King and bishop vs. king and bishop when the bishops are on the same color

Draw procedure

Most draws are draws by mutual agreement. Having played your move, you ask your opponent if they would like a draw. Ask in your own time, before you press the clock button. The opponent may accept your draw offer, in which case the game ends immediately. If they decline your offer, or do not respond, the game continues and your offer is canceled with their next move. Draw offers cannot be withdrawn on that move.

Draw etiquette

Only offer a draw if you believe that the position is drawn. Beginners sometimes offer a draw after they have made a mistake, hoping that their opponent will accept. However, this would be regarded as impertinent because it implies that the opponent is incapable of winning from an advantageous position.

When playing a much stronger player, you should allow them to offer the draw first. They may have a plan which you have not considered. You could also be showing a sign of weakness because being satisfied with a draw indicates that you are no longer trying to win.

There is no official limit on how many draw offers you can make in a game. However, if you make a draw offer after every move, your opponent could complain that you are being distracting, which is against the rules of chess.

Tournament leaders will sometimes ask for a draw even if they are in a superior position if obtaining a draw will secure them a prize, or they may want to save their energy for the next game.

Famous chess players

Here are some of the world's best, and best-known, players.

Historic players

Robert (Bobby) J. Fischer won the 1958 US Championship when he was 14. He won eight times—each time he entered. He became a grandmaster at the age of 15½, the youngest in history. Fischer became the world chess champion in 1972 aged 29 in the most famous chess match in history against the Russian Boris Spassky. He even invented a clock in which extra time is added after each move—a method which has been adopted by the chess world.

Judit Polgár is the strongest female of all time. She became a grandmaster at the age of 15 years and 4 months, beating Bobby Fischer's record. She won numerous international tournaments, beat 11 world champions including Magnus Carlsen, and was rated in the top ten players in the world. With a rating over 2700, she was a super grandmaster before she retired in 2015. Judit is the youngest of three sisters, all of them chess prodigies. By practicing and studying chess positions every day, they mastered the game.

Vera Menchik became the first women's world champion in 1927. She was never defeated, and remained world champion for the rest of her life, proving she could beat the top male players. Tragically, in 1944, she was killed in the Blitz on London in World War II. She is remembered in the trophy for the winning team in the women's chess Olympiad: it's called the Vera Menchik Cup.

Today's players

Magnus Carlsen (born 1990) from Norway started playing chess at the age of 5 and became a grandmaster at 13⅓! He became world champion in 2013 at the age of 23. He has been the top-rated player in the world since he was 19, and is the highest rated player of all time at over 2800. He says that he is now more interested in trying to reach 2900 than to keep winning titles. He's also the richest chess player in the world due to his prize money, sponsorship deals, and setting up his own software company.

Carissa Yip (born 2003) learned the game aged 6, and defeated a grandmaster when she was 10, the youngest female ever to beat a grandmaster. She was USA girls' champion three times. She became a Woman Grandmaster when she was 16 and was the youngest American female to gain the International Master title in 2020. She won the 2021 US women's championship at age 18 and is the top-rated female in the USA at over 2400. Carissa always completes her homework before chess—she studies chess for half an hour a day by practicing tactical puzzles.

Alireza Firouzja (born 2003) is the youngest ever player with a rating of over 2800. He started playing chess at the age of 8, won the Iranian championship aged 12, and became a grandmaster at 14. He is the second highest rated player in the world behind Magnus Carlsen. He left Iran because of their policies against Israeli players. He moved to France where he plays for their national team. Magnus Carlsen has suggested that Alireza could be a future world champion.

CHESS & TECHNOLOGY

It's great to play with physical pieces on a board against another person...but most chess games are played online.

There are lots of advantages to playing online. You can play whenever you like. There will always be someone of your level to play against. You can play people from all over the world. Millions of games are played every week. To make progress in chess, you will need to engage in online play at some point.

Most online games are played fast—either 5 minutes or less per player per game for all moves (Blitz Chess) or 3 minutes or less per game (Bullet Chess). Such fast play calls upon memory and instinct rather than allowing time for a careful analysis of a position.

Advanced Tip

The rules of chess are slightly different when you play online. Instead of claiming a draw for threefold repetition of the position, the platform automatically declares a draw after 50 moves.

As a beginner, you'll need a slower time control—between 15 minutes and 30 minutes per person per game.

Games can be casual or rated. A casual game is suitable just for practice. Rated games are for measuring how your performance increases (or decreases) over time. You can play anonymously, but if you want to store your results you need to register—always ask a parent or guardian before you do.

The online platforms take cheating seriously. They compare your moves with a chess engine. If your moves are so good that even the world champion would not find them, then you're suspected of cheating. This could mean a suspension or a ban from playing on the platform.

Online chess platforms

There are several very good chess platforms for young people. Here are two of the most popular.

ChessKid (ChessKid.com) is an American-based company which offers everything a budding player needs.

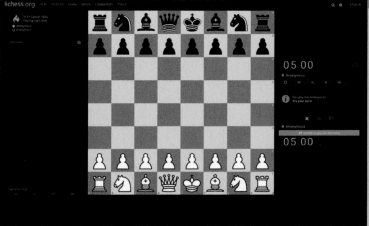

Lichess (Lichess.org) is a free, open-source platform run by a non-profit organization in France. Programmers from around the world volunteer to develop the platform.

Playing computers

On May 11th, 1997, the IBM supercomputer Deep Blue beat the world champion, Gary Kasparov. From that date, computers have been recognized as being able to play stronger chess than humans.

Above: Gary Kasparov playing Deep Blue in 1997

Nowadays, smartphones are much more powerful than the Deep Blue computer. This is useful for analyzing your games afterward to find out where you went wrong.

We call the collection of algorithms which figure out the best chess move a "chess engine." Chess engines work by generating numerous variations, and then evaluating the resulting positions.

Some devious people have secretly used their smartphone to check their moves during a game. Many tournaments now have restrictions on carrying smartphones, especially while a chess game is in progress. For top level competitions, the players are scanned as they enter the playing area to make sure that they have no digital devices.

Famous chess engines

Stockfish is the best known of the traditional engines. It's free and open-source. Under development since 2008, it has won the world championship of chess engines on multiple occasions. It can be installed on any device.

Alpha Zero started the new generation of chess engines in 2017 using neural network algorithms. Developed by DeepMind, the artificial intelligence team at Google, it runs millions of games to work out winning moves.

DecodeChess is an "explanatory engine." Most chess engines advise the best move, but can't explain *why* it is the best. Explanatory engines like DecodeChess try to explain why a move has been chosen.

The mechanical chess player

In 1770, a chess-playing machine called the Mechanical Turk wowed the world. It consisted of a life-size model of the top half of a man. He had a beard and was dressed like a sorcerer, sitting in front of a large cabinet with drawers and shelves.

When the operator opened these, the audience would see an elaborate set of gears and pulleys, giving the impression of a clockwork mechanism. People would challenge the machine to a game, but would usually lose. The Turk moved the pieces with its arm.

But it was all a hoax. The machine had a secret compartment in which a chess player sat!

The Mechanical Turk caused a sensation in Vienna where it was launched. The machine went on tour in Europe. Benjamin Franklin, the American ambassador to Paris, was impressed, and even Napoleon played it. The machine was exhibited in America from 1826 and was finally destroyed in a fire in Philadelphia in 1854. Nobody ever found out about the secret of its success until afterward, when the story was told.

Chess databases

Every competitive game must be recorded. Chess event organizers publish these games to promote their events. Chess players like to look at these games to find novel moves and ideas. In advance of a competitive game, players will look up a chess database and review past games by their opponents to find out what openings and defenses they play, and to note strengths and weaknesses.

It is advisable to start keeping your own record of your games in a chess scorebook. After each game, analyze the moves and write down your thoughts. This will prove to be invaluable subsequently when you want to ascertain whether you are making progress. Write down not just any move analysis but also your reflections on your state of mind. Did you move too quickly? Were you too optimistic? Did you underestimate your opponent?

You will put a lot of effort into your games—the preparation, the playing, and the post-game analysis. To obtain the greatest benefit you should keep the games in a chess database. This will allow you to call up games, to analyze your opening repertoire, and to find out your strengths and weaknesses. Most importantly, you can compare your moves with those of the experts. The chess databases store millions of games.

Most chess databases incorporate a chess engine so that you can analyze the games in the same place as you store them. There is a facility for printing out your games with diagrams if you want to publish your game in a school or club magazine.

The best databases

ChessBase is a database running on a PC with special features for use by grandmasters. ChessBase comes with its own chess engine, Fritz.

Hiarcs is a database and engine which runs on a PC and Mac. It provides all the features required for a club player.

PORTABLE GAME NOTATION

The standard file format for storing chess games is in a text format with the suffix ".pgn" standing for Portable Game Notation. For instance, the .pgn file for The Paris Opera Game, played in 1858 between Paul Morphy against the Duke of Brunswick and Count Isouard, looks like this.

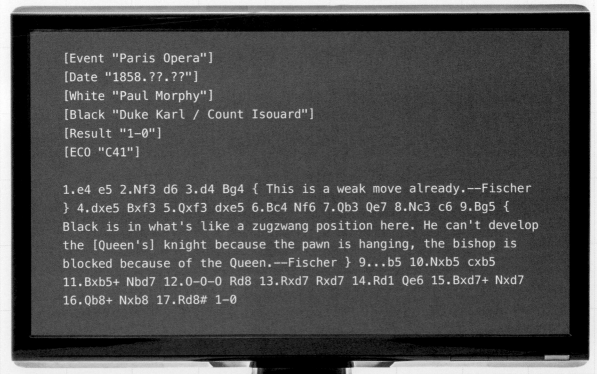

```
[Event "Paris Opera"]
[Date "1858.??.??"]
[White "Paul Morphy"]
[Black "Duke Karl / Count Isouard"]
[Result "1-0"]
[ECO "C41"]

1.e4 e5 2.Nf3 d6 3.d4 Bg4 { This is a weak move already.--Fischer
} 4.dxe5 Bxf3 5.Qxf3 dxe5 6.Bc4 Nf6 7.Qb3 Qe7 8.Nc3 c6 9.Bg5 {
Black is in what's like a zugzwang position here. He can't develop
the [Queen's] knight because the pawn is hanging, the bishop is
blocked because of the Queen.--Fischer } 9...b5 10.Nxb5 cxb5
11.Bxb5+ Nbd7 12.0-0-0 Rd8 13.Rxd7 Rxd7 14.Rd1 Qe6 15.Bxd7+ Nxd7
16.Qb8+ Nxb8 17.Rd8# 1-0
```

SHIROV vs. POLGÁR

This is a game played between grandmasters Alexei Shirov (Latvia) and Judit Polgár (Hungary) played at Buenos Aires (Argentina) in 1994. Alexei Shirov was the third ranked player in the world. Judit became a grandmaster at the age of 15 and is regarded as the strongest female chess player of all time, having beaten ten world champions!

Alexei Shirov

v

Judit Polgár

1   1.e4 c5

The Sicilian is a combative defense that leads to dynamic positions.

2   2.Nf3 e6 3.d4 cxd4 4.Nxd4 Nc6

The Taimanov Variation of the Sicilian which plays the knight to a natural square. (Mark Taimanov was a Ukrainian grandmaster.)

3   5.Nc3 d6 6.g4 a6

6.g4 is an aggressive move. Shirov means business.

6..a6 is a useful waiting move with several purposes. It stops a knight from going to **b5** attacking **d6** and **c7** if the black queen moves there. It also makes possible **b5** to allow the **c8** bishop to go to **b7**.

4   7.Be3 Nge7 8.Nb3 b5 9.f4 Bb7 10.Qf3

Judit avoids developing the king's knight to **f6** because it would be chased away by **g5**. The bishop on **b7** eyes the queen and rook on the long diagonal. White is building up a strong attacking formation with three pawns advancing toward the king and the queen looking at the unprotected rook at **a8**. Black is in danger of being crushed but Judit has prepared a riposte.

5   10...g5! 11.fxg5 Ne5

Judit has sacrificed a pawn so that she can get her knight to **e5**. This is a splendid outpost because no pawn can attack the knight and it stops the pawn advances to **e5** and **g6**. It also gains a tempo by attacking the queen which is forced to move to **g2** to protect **e4**.

6   12.Qg2 b4 13.Ne2 h5!

Another pawn sacrifice. Judit wants her other knight to spring into action and gets rid of the pawn preventing this. In dynamic chess positions, the activity of the pieces counts for more than the material balance.

7   14.gxh5 Nf5 15.Bf2

White's **g4** pawn, which was guarding the **f5** square, has been diverted, allowing the knight on **e7** to jump to **f5**. The **e4** pawn is pinned against the queen by the bishop on **b7**. White meekly retreats his threatened bishop to **f2**. Now comes another great move.

8   15...Qxg5!

Judit grabs back a pawn and offers the queen. It is a decoy sacrifice because if White captures the queen **16 QxQ** then Black has the royal fork **16...Nf3+ 17.Kd1 Nxg5** with a big advantage because the **e4** pawn is now pinned against the **h1** rook and will be lost along with the **h5** pawn. Black's pieces are better coordinated.

9   16.Na5 Ne3!

Shirov declines the offer and goes after the pesky bishop which is causing so much trouble with **16.Na5**.

Judit finds another forcing move, dropping the knight into the heart of Black's position and attacking the queen again.

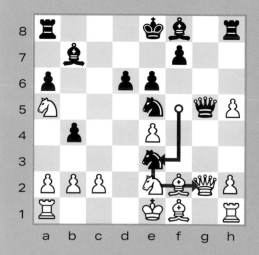

10   Variation: 17.QxQ Nf3

White still cannot capture the queen because of **17.QxQ Nf3** checkmate. This would be the remarkable checkmate position.

White avoids this variation and offers to exchange queens on **g3**.

11   17.Qg3 Qxg3 18.Nxg3 Nxc2+

Judit sees that after the exchange of queens, the knight can fork White's king and rook.

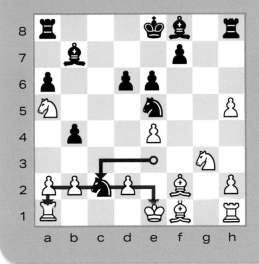

12   19.Kd1 Nxa1 20.Nxb7 b3 21.axb3 Nxb3

Even though White captures the **b7** bishop, Black wins a rook. The knight in the **a1** corner has a neat way to extricate itself. The net result is that Black has "won the exchange" i.e. has a rook for a minor piece.

13   2.Kc2 Nc5 23.Nxc5 dxc5 24.Be1 Nf3 25.Bc3 Nd4+

Judit maneuvers her knight from **e5** to the outpost on **d4**. Approaching the endgame, Black has a clear advantage once the rooks are brought into action.

14   26.Kd3 Bd6 27.Bg2 Be5 28.Kc4 Ke7 29.Ra1 Nc6 0-1

Black has had enough and resigns. An immortal game by Judit Polgár.

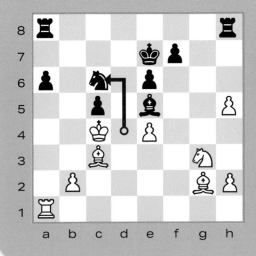

GLOSSARY

50 Move Rule
A player can claim a draw if no capture has been made and no pawn has been moved in the last fifty consecutive moves.

Absolute pin
A pin against the king, called absolute because the pinned piece cannot legally move as it would expose the king to check.

Active
Describes a piece that is able to move or control many squares.

Adjournment
Suspension of a chess game with the intention to continue at a later occasion.

Adjudication
The process of deciding on the outcome of an unfinished game. This is usually undertaken by a strong player and may involve chess analysis software.

Adjust
When a player does not intend to move a piece, but to slightly move the piece to center it on a square, the player first says, "I adjust" (or j'adoube in international play), and then adjusts that piece. Otherwise, the touch-move rule applies. Adjustment can only be done when it is the player's move.

Advantage
When a player is superior to their opponent in material, space, time, or pawn structure.

Analysis
Study of a position to determine best play for both sides.

Announced mate
Where one player announces check a sequence of moves, leading to a forced checkmate in a specified number of moves (for example, "mate in three").

Attack
A sequence of moves often in a particular formation designed to checkmate "mating attack" against the enemy king or a minority attack against the opponent's queenside pawn structure.

Attack Power
The attack power of a piece is the total of the opponent's squares being attacked after the piece completes its move.

B
Symbol used for the bishop when recording chess moves in English.

Back rank
A player's first rank (the one on which the pieces stand in the initial array); White's back rank is Black's eighth rank and vice versa.

Back-rank mate
A checkmate given by a queen or rook along the back rank with the opponent's king blocked in by its own pawns.

Backward pawn
A pawn that cannot be supported by other pawns because it is behind them. (Relating to pawns of the same color on the adjacent files).

Bad bishop
A bishop which is hemmed in by its own pawns.

Battery
Two pieces attacking along the same file, rank, or diagonal (queen and rook, two rooks, or queen and bishop) putting pressure on the defense.

Bishops on opposite colors
A situation in which one side has only its light-squared bishop remaining while the other has only its dark-squared bishop remaining. In endgames, this often results in a draw if there are no other pieces (only pawns), since the bishops control different squares.

Blindfold chess
A form of chess in which one or both players are not allowed to see the board.

Blitz chess
Chess with 5 minutes per player for the entire game. (Blitz is German for lightning.)

Blockade
The placement of a piece directly in front of an enemy pawn, where it restrains the pawn's advance and gains shelter from attack.

Blunder
A serious mistake or oversight which loses the game or throws away the advantage. Indicated by "??" in notation.

Brilliancy
A spectacular and beautiful game of chess, generally featuring sacrificial attacks and unexpected moves. Brilliancies are not always required to feature sound play or the best moves by either side.

Calculate
To carefully plan a series of moves while considering possible responses.

Candidate move

A move that seems good upon initial observation of the position.

Capture

Also known as "take." Your piece moves onto the square on which your opponent's piece was sitting and then you take their piece off of the board. This is usually in one motion. See also *en passant*.

Castle

Castling is a special move when the king is moved two squares toward a rook and then the rook moves to the other side of the king. See p34 for more information. Castling on the kingside is sometimes called castling short and castling on the queenside is called castling long.

Center

The center comprises the four squares (**d4**, **e5**, **e4**, and **e5**) in the middle of the board.

Central control

Having one or more pieces that attack any of the four center squares. One of the main aims from the opening.

Centralize

A central placing of a piece so that it can attack numerous squares of the opponent and is available for play on either flank.

Central pawn

A pawn on the king's file or queen's file, i.e. on the d-file or e-file.

Check

When a piece or pawn is attacking the opponent's king, then that king is said to be in "check." You may declare "check" but experienced players rarely need to do so.

Checkmate

When a player is in "check" and has no legal move to escape from "check" whether by moving

the king, blocking the attack, or capturing the attacker. A player whose king is checkmated loses the game.

Chessboard

The checkered board used in chess consisting of 64 squares (eight rows and eight columns) arranged in two alternating colors (light and dark).

Closed file

A file on which Black and White both have a pawn.

Closed game

A position with few open lines (files or diagonals), interlocking pawn chains (typically six files contain pawns of both colors), and cramped positions with few opportunities to exchange. It often arises from the opening **1.d4 d5**.

Combination

A series of two or more moves to gain the advantage. Each move forces your opponent to make a specific response.

Connected passed pawns

Passed pawns on adjacent files. These are very powerful if they can advance together.

Connected pawns

Two or more of one player's pawns that are on adjacent files.

Connected rooks

Two rooks of the same color on the same rank or file with no pawns or pieces between them. Connected rooks are desirable because the rooks support each other.

Counterattack

An attack that responds to an attack by the other player.

Counterplay

When a player with a positional disadvantage makes moves that cannot be ignored.

Dark squares

The 32 dark-colored squares on the chessboard, such as **a1** and **h8**. A dark square is always located at a player's left-hand corner.

Dark-square bishop

One of the two bishops that moves on the dark squares, situated in **c1** and **f8** in the initial position.

Dead draw

A drawn position in which neither player has any realistic chance to win.

Decoy

A move that lures an opponent's piece away to an unfavorable square e.g. so that it can be trapped.

Defense

Placing your pieces in positions which will make it hard for your opponent to attack your king or penetrate behind your pawns. Also refers to the opening played by Black.

Deflection

Any move which lures the opponent's defending piece away from that which is being defended, usually as part of a combination.

Development

The process of moving pieces from their starting position.

Diagonal

A line of squares of the same color touching corner to corner, along which a queen or bishop can move such as **a1** to **h8**.

Discovered attack

An attack by a queen, rook or bishop when another piece or pawn moves out of its way.

Discovered check

A discovered attack to the king

Double attack
Two attacks made with one move: these attacks may be made by the same piece (in which case it is a fork); or by different pieces (a situation which may arise via a discovered attack in which the moved piece also makes a threat). The attacks may directly threaten opposing pieces, or may be threats of another kind: for instance, to capture the queen and deliver checkmate.

Double check
A check delivered by two pieces at the same time. The only possible defense to a double check is for the king to move.

Doubled pawns
Two pawns of the same color on the same file.

Doubled rooks
Two of a player's rooks placed on the same file or rank.

Draw
A game in which neither player wins and both players share the point(s). See p92 for more.

Elo rating system
A method for calculating the relative skill levels of chess players. Above 2000 is an expert. Grandmasters need to be at least 2500 to qualify. The World Champion is over 2800.

En passant
The rule that allows a pawn that has just advanced two squares to be captured by a pawn on the same rank and adjacent file. From the French term meaning "in passing". See p37 for more information.

Endgame
The third and final phase of a Chess game. Beginning when just a few pieces are left on the board or a winning attack begins on the opponent's king.

Engine
Software algorithm which calculates the best move to play.

Escape square
A square to which a piece can move, which allows it to escape attack. Also known as "luft" (German for "air").

Exchange
The mutual capture of a pair of pieces, one white and the other black, usually of the same type, or of bishop for knight (two pieces that are considered almost equal in value).

Exchange sacrifice
Giving up a rook for a minor piece.

Expert
An experienced player, especially one with an Elo rating above 2000.

FIDE
"Federation Internationale des Echecs," the International Chess Federation. Pronounced "fee-day".

File
A vertical column of eight squares, signified by a letter (a through h).

Flank
The a,b,c files on the queenside and the f,g,h files on the kingside. (Also "wing")

Fool's Mate
The shortest possible game which is as follows: **1. f3 e5, 2. g4 Qh5#**.

Forced move
A move which is the only one which does not result in a serious disadvantage for the moving player. "Forced" can also be used to describe a sequence of moves for which the player has no viable alternative, e.g. "the forced win of a piece" or "a forced checkmate."

Fork
When one piece (usually a knight) or a pawn attacks two enemy pieces at the same time. A form of double attack. The fork of a King and Queen is a Royal Fork. The fork of a King, Queen, and Rook is a Family Fork.

Gambit
The voluntary sacrifice of a pawn in the opening moves in order to get a compensating advantage in space or development.

Grandmaster (GM)
The highest title awarded by FIDE to a player.

Half-open file
A file on which only one player has no pawns.

Hanging
Placing a piece/pawn on a square where it can be captured without compensation.

Hanging pawns
Two pawns next to each other which can't be protected by other pawns.

Hole
Any square which cannot be defended by a pawn.

Illegal move
A move that is not permitted by the rules of chess. An illegal move discovered during the course of a game is to be corrected.

Illegal position
A position in a game that is a consequence of an illegal move or an incorrect starting position.

International Master (IM)
A title awarded by FIDE to a player. This level is above Master and below Grandmaster.

Isolated pawn
A pawn that has no pawns of the same color on adjacent files (AKA isolani when it is the Q pawn).

K
Symbol used for the king when recording chess moves in English.

King hunt
A series of moves that chase the enemy king all over the board until it is mated.

King's bishop
The bishop that was on the king-side at the start of the game. The terms King's Knight and King's Rook are also used. Sometimes abbreviated KB, KN, and KR respectively. The king pawn is the pawn on the king's file.

Kingside
The half of the board made up of the e,f,g,h files.

Legal move
Moving a piece according to the laws of chess.

Light squares
The 32 light-colored squares on the chessboard, such as **h1** and **a8**.

Light-square bishop
One of the two bishops moving on the light squares, situated on **f1** or **c8** in the initial position.

Line
(a) An open path for a piece (queen, rook, or bishop) to move or control squares.

(b) A sequence of moves, usually in the opening or in analyzing a position.

Liquidation
Capturing pieces to simplify the position and make it easier to promote a pawn or checkmate the opponent.

Long diagonal
One of the two diagonals with eight squares (**a1-h8** or **h1-a8**), the longest on the board.

Major pieces
Collective term for queen and rooks (AKA heavy pieces).

Majority
A larger number of pawns on one flank opposed by a smaller number of the opponent's. Often a player with a majority on one flank has a minority on the other.

Master
A player with an Elo rating between 2200 and 2399.

Mate
Short for checkmate.

Material
All of a player's pieces and pawns on the board. The player with pieces and pawns of greater value is said to have a "material advantage".

Mating attack
An attack against an opponent's king that is intended to lead to checkmate.

Mating net
An attack against the king using multiple pieces leading to checkmate in a few moves.

Middlegame
The phase of the game between the Opening and Endgame.

Minor pieces
The collective term for bishops and knights.

Minority attack
An attack of two or more connected pawns against the opponent's majority of connected pawns, usually carried out to provoke a weakness.

N
Symbol used for the knight when recording chess moves in English.

Notation
The recording of each move by both players in a chess game.

Occupation
When a queen or rook controls a file or rank.

0-0
The symbol for kingside castling.

0-0-0
The symbol for queenside castling.

Open file
A vertical column of eight squares that is free of pawns. (See also "half-open" file.)

Opening
The beginning of a game. The basic goals are to develop pieces quickly and control as much of the center as possible with pawns and pieces and find protection for the king.

Openings
Established sequences of moves played at the beginning of the game.

Opposite-colored bishops
When each player has pawns and has as their only piece a bishop, and the bishops are not operating on the same colored squares. This type of endgame usually ends in a draw.

Orthodox chess
Standard chess played according to the Laws of Chess. Distinguished from a chess "variant."

Outside passed pawn
A passed pawn that is near the edge of the board and far away from other pawns. In the endgame, such a pawn often constitutes a strong advantage for its owner.

Over-the-board (OTB) chess
Chess played face-to-face, as opposed to on the internet.

Passed pawn
A pawn that has no pawn of the opposite color on its file or on any adjacent files on its way to queening.

Passive
A piece that is able to move to or control relatively few squares, or a position with several such pieces. (Also referred to as an "inactive.")

Pawn chain
Three or more pawns in a diagonal line with each protected by a pawn behind it on an adjacent file, and blocked by an enemy pawn directly ahead.

Pawn storm
An attacking technique where a group of pawns on one wing is advanced to break up the defense.

Pawn structure
All aspects of pawn placement. The position of the pawns greatly influences the character of the game.

Perpetual check
A draw forced by one player putting the opponent's king in a potentially endless series of checks

Pin
When a piece is attacked and cannot move without losing a piece of greater value. When the piece of greater value is the king it is an absolute pin, when it is a piece other than the king it is called a relative pin.

Plan
A clear idea of what moves you want to play taking into account your opponent's likely responses. Typically expressed as a sequence of if-then statements.

Point count
A system that gives the pieces the following numeric values: Queen = 9, Rook = 5, Bishop = 3, Knight = 3, and Pawn = 1.

Poisoned pawn/piece
An unprotected pawn/piece that, if captured, would lead to a serious disadvantage for the player capturing the pawn/piece.

Promotion
When a pawn reaches the 8th rank, it can be promoted to a queen (or sometimes another piece—see under-promotion)

Q
Symbol used for the queen when recording chess moves in English.

Queen pawn
The pawn in front of the queen.

Queenside
The half of the board that includes the a,b,c,d files.

R
Symbol used for the rook when recording chess moves in English.

Rank
A horizontal row of eight squares, signified by a number (1 through 8). Rank names are always given from the point of view of each individual player, with the first rank being the home row of the king and other pieces.

Rapid chess (or rapidplay)
Each player has 30 minutes to make all of their moves.

Removal of the guard
This is a chess tactic in which a defensive piece is captured, leaving one of the opponent's pieces undefended or underdefended.

Resign
To concede loss of the game because checkmate is inevitable.

Rook pawn
A pawn on the rook's file.

Round
A round is when one player plays another player in a tournament. There will be a series of rounds in the tournament.

Sacrifice
Voluntarily giving up pieces for better space, time, or for a mating attack. (Sometimes abbreviated to "sac").

Scholar's mate
A four-move checkmate common among beginners in which White plays **1. e4**, followed by **Qh5** (or **Qf3**) and **Bc4**, mating with **4. Qxf7#**.

Score
A record of the moves of a particular game, usually expressed in algebraic notation.

Score sheet
The sheet of paper used to record a game in process. During competitive games, both players must record the game using a score sheet.

Sharp play
Risky, double-edged, and highly tactical play.

Simplify
To trade off pieces of equal value to try to get fewer pieces on the board. A player who has an advantage (more or stronger pieces) will usually want to do this to reduce counterplay.

Skewer
An attack to a valuable piece, compelling it to move to avoid capture and exposing a less valuable piece which can then be taken.

Space
The number of squares controlled by a player.

Stalemate

When it is a player's move and they have no legal moves and not in check. A stalemate results in an immediate draw.

Staunton chessmen

The standard design of chess pieces, required for use in competitions.

Strategy

The reasoning behind a longer term plan. Typically making best use of their advantages in a specific position while minimizing the impact of their positional disadvantages.

Sudden death

The most straightforward time control for a chess game: each player has a fixed amount of time available to make all moves.

Tactics

Play characterized by short-term attacks and threats giving one player an advantage in pieces or position, often requiring extensive calculation by the players. Tactics include pins, sacrifices, skewers, decoys, and deflections.

Tempo

One move. If a piece can reach a useful square in one move, but takes two moves to get there, it has lost a tempo.

Threat

A plan or move that, if left unattended, would result in an immediate depreciation of the opponent's position or material

Threefold repetition of position

This is a draw which occurs when all of the pieces of both players have been in the same position at three times during the game. From the first occurrence of this position to the last, no pieces can have been captured and there must be an accurate score sheet proving the repetition. The repetition does not have to be in consecutive moves.

Time control

The amount of time each player has to play the game or make a specified number of moves.

Time pressure

When a player has several moves left before reaching a time control or there are less than five minutes left in a sudden-death game.

Touch-move rule

The rule that if a player touches a piece then that piece must be moved, if moving that piece is a legal move. See p88 for more.

Tournament

A competition between chess players, divided up into rounds.

Trap

Luring an opponent into making a poor move.

Under-promotion

When a pawn reaches the last rank and promotes to any piece other than a queen.

Unpin

A counterattack that breaks a pin, gains time to break a pin, or ends a pin by eliminating (takes) or diverting (forcing to move) a pinning unit.

Variant

A chesslike game played using a different board, pieces, or rules than orthodox chess.

Variation

One line of analysis (i.e. a different move) for any move of a game. Usually applied to the openings

Winning the exchange

The exchange is used to refer to the advantage of a rook over a minor piece (knight or bishop). The player who captures a rook while losing a minor piece is said to have won the exchange, and the opponent is said to have lost the exchange.

Zugzwang

A situation in the endgame in which a player has no good moves or waiting moves, so they must make a move to their disadvantage.

Zwischenschach

A zwischenzug that is a check. (German.)

Zwischenzug

An in-between move. A move played before the expected reply, which usually delivers a threat. (German, pronounced "zwishen-tsoog.")

Acknowledgments

This book derives from the Smart Method developed by ChessPlus using games to develop thinking skills.

www.chessplus.net

International Master Jesper Hall, a former coach to the young Magnus Carlsen, provided pedagogical insights. Brigitta Peszleg provided philosophical insights. Rita Atkins showed the importance of flexible diagram creation using the Logiqboard.

The book could not have been written without my wife Leila's moral support and copious cups of tea.

About the author

John Foley is Former London Junior Under-16 Chess Champion and Oxford University Chess Champion.

He is the Director of ChessPlus Ltd, the games education consultancy. He has authored many books, workbooks and articles on chess, including *21 Strategy Games for the Chessboard*, *50 Chess and Mathematics Exercises*, and many more.

The publishers would like to thank the following sources for their kind permission to reproduce the pictures in this book.

GETTY IMAGES: Page 94: (top right) Bettmann, (left) Yves Forestier/Sygma, (bottom right) William Vanderson/Fox Photos/Hulton Archive; Page 95: (top right) Dan Kitwood, (left) Jonathan Wiggs/The Boston Globe, (bottom right) Miguel Pereira; Page 98: Al Tielemans /Sports Illustrated; Page 99: (bottom right) ZU_09; Page 102: (left) Jaime Reina/AFP, (right) Chip Hires/Gamma-Rapho.

SHUTTERSTOCK: ojos de hojalata/Shutterstock.com, Motortion Films/Shutterstock.com, Rupesh A. Nalawade/Shutterstock.com, Den Rozhnovsky/Shutterstock.com, Trofimova Vika/Shutterstock.com, Twin Design/Shutterstock.com, SAKARET TAWAKOON/Shutterstock.com, cigdem/Shutterstock.com, namaki/Shutterstock.com, Pixel-Shot/Shutterstock.com, LINGTREN.COM/Shutterstock.com, Alexandr III/Shutterstock.com, Mario De Moya F/Shutterstock.com, Golden Sikorka/Shutterstock.com, Jamesbin/Shutterstock.com, VikiVector/Shutterstock.com, FAMILY STOCK/Shutterstock.com

Every effort has been made to acknowledge correctly and contact the source and/or copyright holder of each picture. Any unintentional errors or omissions will be corrected in future editions of this book.